THE
CATECHIST'S
TOOLBOX

JOE PAPROCKI

THE CATECHIST'S TOOLBOX

How to Thrive as a Religious Education Teacher

Skills, Tips, and Practical Advice You Can Use Today

LOYOLAPRESS.

CHICAGO

LOYOLAPRESS.

3441 N. Ashland Avenue
Chicago, Illinois 60657
(800) 621-1008
WWW.LOYOLABOOKS.ORG

Portions of this book were previously published in Tools for Teaching: Classroom Tips for Catechists (Mystic, CT: Twenty-third Publications, 1997).

Cover design by Tracy Sainz
Interior design by Loyola Press

Library of Congress Cataloging-in-Publication Data

Paprocki, Joe.
    The catechist's toolbox : how to thrive as a religious education teacher : skills, tips, and practical advice you can use now / Joe Paprocki.
        p. cm.
    ISBN-13: 978-0-8294-2451-5
    ISBN-10: 0-8294-2451-2
    1. Catechetics—Catholic Church. 2. Catechists. 3. Christian education—Teaching methods. 4. Catholic Church—Education. I. Title.
    BX1968.P377 2007
    268'.6—dc22

                                                    2007007178

Printed in the United States of America
07 08 09 10 11 12 RRD 10 9 8 7 6 5 4 3 2

To Jo, Mike, and Amy, whose love has brought immeasurable "home improvement" to my life.

CONTENTS

ACKNOWLEDGMENTS

I would like to thank the people at Loyola Press for allowing me the opportunity to place my gifts at the service of those who form the cate-chetical community. Special thanks to Joe Durepos for generating such excitement over this project.

★ ★

A catechist is a person who facilitates the process of faith formation. This is done first by echoing the word of God in his or her own life, and second by helping others to do so. Please know that you are not easily replaced. Although there may be a half-million volunteer catechists in the United States, you are part of a select community of people in the church who are dedicated to sharing the Good News of Jesus Christ in a formal setting. Through your work with adults, families, adolescents, and children, you are passing on a lived faith.

★ ★

On-the-Job Training

Imagine that you are moving into a house or an apartment. There's a great deal of work to be done, isn't there? Aside from moving all your personal belongings and furniture, you find that there are many repairs and improvements to be accomplished before you can move a single thing into your new home. If you're like most people, you compromise: some of the work gets done by professionals, while much of it is accomplished by you with on-the-job training.

> Like a home improvement manual, *The Catechist's Toolbox* is a do-it-yourself manual to provide you, the volunteer catechist, with on-the-job training and assistance.

At one time or another, all of us have tried to undertake some home repairs by ourselves. Manuals can be very helpful in assisting the novice home-repair person in tackling some projects that otherwise would require much more time and money if handled by a professional. By following the step-by-step instructions, we are able to do some minor plumbing, electrical work, and even construction. Accomplishing these tasks, however, is not a reason to give up our day jobs. To be certified as a professional plumber, electrician, or construction worker takes a great deal of time, experience, studying, and preparation.

On-the-Job Training for Catechists

As catechists, many of us find ourselves face-to-face with challenges for which we have had no formal training. Most of us are not professional schoolteachers with training in methods and skills for classroom management. What are we to do? For the most part, we will have to discover on our own how to handle certain situations and challenges. Like a home-improvement manual, *The Catechist's Toolbox* is a do-it-yourself manual to provide you, the volunteer catechist, with on-the-job training and assistance.

No Shortcuts!

The truth is, in order to be an effective catechist, you need more than good intentions. Think about it: electricians and plumbers must complete thousands of hours of training before being certified. It makes sense that catechists—people who are entrusted with the spiritual formation of children, young people, and adults—should likewise be required to complete training and formation leading to certification in their local diocese. *The Catechist's Toolbox* is not meant to be a substitute for formal catechetical formation and training. Rather, it is meant to complement such preparation so that you can become the effective catechist that God is calling you to be.

Chapter One

Shop-talk: The Language
of Catechesis

I enjoy browsing around the local home improvement/hardware megastore, allowing myself to get lost in the vast array of gizmos, gadgets, and thingamajigs. I've just tipped my hand to a problem that I have—I don't always know the correct names of the items that I'm looking for. Often, when a store worker comes up to me and asks if I need some help, I feel embarrassed. I know what I'm looking for but I don't know the correct name. Relying on gestures to describe the shape, size, and purpose of the item I need, I end up feeling like I don't speak the same language as the worker. Eventually, he or she figures out what it is that I'm looking for, the purchase is completed, and I can get back to my home improvement project.

> "Catechetical materials... should encourage and assist in the development of a common language of faith within the Church."
>
> *National Directory for Catechesis*, 70A

The Language of Faith Formation

Home improvement has a language of its own. The same is true of faith formation. In fact, in many ways, the church has a language of its own.

For our purposes, we need to become more familiar with the language of faith formation, or catechetical language.

The church seems to like big words. Here are a few you probably don't use in everyday conversation!

- ◆ Ecclesiology
- ◆ Evangelization
- ◆ Magisterium
- ◆ Transubstantiation

- ◆ Episcopacy
- ◆ Sanctification
- ◆ Ecumenism

In decades past, the church did such a good job of teaching us a language of faith formation for children (CCD) that we are still having a difficult time of growing beyond this term.

Since the Second Vatican Council, the church has been emphasizing a different set of words in relation to faith formation or religious education. Notice that I did not refer to these words as new. The fact is, the words that the church is now using when it comes to faith formation are words that are actually quite ancient. They may seem new to many of us but to the church, they are more like antiques.

It doesn't take a rocket scientist to realize that all of these words derive from the same root word—the Greek word *katakein* meaning "to echo" or "to sound again." When one person echoes another, it means that he or she is imitating or reflecting back what that person has said or done. So what do each of these words mean?

Do you know what CCD stands for?

Confraternity of Christian Doctrine

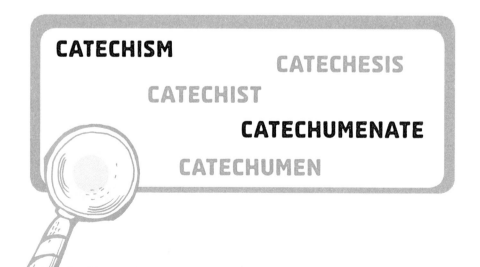

CATECHISM

CATECHESIS

CATECHIST

CATECHUMENATE

CATECHUMEN

➕ **A catechism is a written summary of the church's understanding of God's word as revealed through Scripture and Tradition.** In a sense, a catechism is the WHAT of our beliefs as Catholics. For many centuries, it was customary for children to "learn their catechism," often through a question-and-answer format known as the *Baltimore Catechism*. Today, the *Catechism of the Catholic Church* (1992) is the official source for Catholic teaching, intended as the principle resource for bishops and catechetical ministers.

For the average adult Catholic, the bishops of the United States have provided the *Compendium of the Catholic Catechism* (2006—a synopsis of the Catholic faith in a question and answer format reminiscent of the *Baltimore Catechism* but for adults) and the *United States Catholic Catechism for Adults* (2006—an adaptation of the *Catechism of the Catholic Church* with stories, teachings, sidebars, cultural applications, reflection questions, and prayer).

➕ **Catechesis is the process of transmitting the gospel.** To help us understand this process, the church has given us the *General Directory for Catechesis* (1997) and the *National Directory for Catechesis* (2005). These documents help us to understand the HOW of catechesis.

➕ **A catechumen is an adult (or child of catechetical age) who is preparing for baptism.** Each Lent, we pattern our lives in such a way as to journey with the catechumens to baptism. Like them, we pray, fast, and give alms as we strive to surrender ourselves to the grace of the death and resurrection of Jesus. The catechumens teach all of us about the desire, commitment, and discipline needed to be a disciple of Jesus.

★ ★

WHATEVER HAPPENED TO CCD?

So, why use the term *catechesis* when we had just gotten used to the term *CCD*? The fact is, *CCD* primarily refers to something that is for children, as well as something that one completes after a given time of study. Today, we have retrieved the notion of catechesis to capture the broader mission of the church to proclaim the gospel to all people: adults, youth, and children—in order to "put people in communion with Jesus Christ" (*Catechism of the Catholic Church* #426)— a task that is lifelong.

★ ★

➕ **The catechumenate is the formal period of preparation for catechumens who are preparing for the Sacraments of Initiation—Baptism, Confirmation, and the Eucharist.** Through the catechumenate, those preparing for initiation into the church receive formation and catechesis from catechists and sponsors, which help them enter more deeply into the Catholic way of life.

➕ **A catechist is a person who facilitates the process of faith formation, first by echoing the word of God in his or her own life and second by helping others to do so.** Please know that you are not easily replaced. Although there may be a half-million volunteer catechists in the U.S., you are part of a select community of people in the church who are dedicated to sharing the Good News of Jesus Christ in a formal setting. Catechists work with adults, families, adolescents, and children, passing on a lived faith.

Ever heard of the RCIA?

This acronym stands for the *Rite of Christian Initiation for Adults*. The RCIA is another name for the catechumenate.

You Have a Vocation

The church makes it quite clear that to be a catechist is to have a vocation. The *General Directory for Catechesis* tells us that "The Church awakens and discerns this divine vocation and confers the mission to catechize. The Lord Jesus invites men and women, in a special way, to follow him, teacher and formator of disciples" (GDC 231). Throughout this book, I use the term *catechist* to refer to those who serve in the parish religious education program as well as those who serve as teachers of religion in Catholic schools.

A Catechist's Role Description

As a catechist, you pray for grace and, no doubt, wonder at times what qualifies you to serve in this ministry. The fact is, you've been called because you exhibit (or show potential for developing) the following qualities and skills:

Qualities of an Effective Catechist

> a desire to grow in and share faith

> an awareness of God's grace and the desire to respond to that grace

> a commitment to the church's liturgical and sacramental life and moral teachings

> a strength of character built on patience, responsibility, confidence, and creativity

> a generosity of spirit, a respect for diversity, and a habit of hospitality and inclusion

Knowledge and Skills of a Catechist

> a basic understanding of Catholic teaching, Scripture, and Catholic Tradition

> honest and caring relationships with young people

> effective teaching techniques and strategies

> Faith formation, however, is more than a subject to be taught— it is an invitation to a way of life.

If you are a Catholic schoolteacher, you are responsible for teaching a variety of subjects throughout the day. Faith formation, however, is more than a subject to be taught—it is an invitation to a way of life. By referring to you as a catechist, I want to recognize and affirm your vocation to form disciples of Jesus. To be referred to as a catechist is an honor that the church bestows only on those who have this vocation.

Expanding Our Vocabulary

Words are very powerful. The Gospel of John refers to Jesus as "the Word made flesh" (John 1:14). The language of faith formation is not just a matter of semantics. By using the most appropriate words to describe who we are and what we do, we deepen our own understanding of our share in Jesus' ministry. As catechists, we assist pastors and bishops in guiding people to a living faith. This living faith has a language all its own. We can begin to learn the language of faith by referring to who we are and what we do with the proper terms.

Scripture

"In the beginning was the Word,
and the Word was with God,
and the Word was God. . . .

And the Word became flesh
and made his dwelling
among us,

and we saw his glory,
the glory as of the Father's
only Son,
full of grace and truth."

(JOHN 1:1, 14)

Prayer

Lord Jesus, Word made flesh, thank you for inviting me to proclaim you to others. Thank you for filling my life with your word. Help me to speak a language of faith that will help others to recognize you in their lives and deepen their relationship with you. May your Word echo within my heart and within the hearts of those I teach. Amen.

For an opportunity to companion with other catechists and to nourish our vocation, visit www.catechistsjourney.com.

Chapter Two

Blueprints: Planning and Preparation

Are you like me? When you try to assemble a piece of furniture, a home computer system, or a new toy for your kids, do you try to do so without looking at the instructions? I admit that this is one of my poorest habits. Once, I tried to put together a shiny new tricycle for my daughter on her birthday. Lo and behold, I assembled the whole thing only to find a very large bolt on the floor. For the life of me, I was unable to figure out where it was supposed to go. Then and only then did I pull out the instructions. Much to my dismay, I had left out a very important bolt that literally held the whole tricycle together. I suppose this is why they tell us to read the instructions first.

> "In concrete terms, catechist formation should . . . provide assistance in catechetical planning."
>
> NATIONAL DIRECTORY FOR CATECHESIS, 55E

Planning and Preparation in Catechesis

Can you imagine a builder attempting to construct a house without first looking at the blueprints? What a catastrophe that would be. The blueprints hold the key to constructing something properly. Yet, when it comes to teaching a lesson, we are often tempted to forge ahead without the proper amount of planning and preparation. If we are going to build a foundation of faith for those we teach, we need to read the blueprints.

Spontaneity is nice, but, paradoxically, those who are best at spontaneity have done their homework and are well prepared for whatever may come their way. In other words, it is easier to be spontaneous when you are well prepared. As a catechist, you need to search for the proper balance between spontaneity and following a script. Planning and preparation are the crucial tools that will help you to achieve this balance. These tools are used when you look over the "blueprints" so that you are able to construct lessons that are strong enough to endure any challenges and to overcome any obstacles.

As a student teacher, I was taught that planning and preparation make up 70 percent of the total act of teaching a lesson. Of course, there may be no way to scientifically prove that percentage, but after many years of

> **"Planning and preparation make up 70 percent of the total act of teaching a lesson."**

teaching, I personally found it to be a very valid estimate. Thorough planning and preparation create a framework for the catechist to move forward in the most effective manner, while avoiding or preempting a large variety of discipline problems. An effective catechist is one who examines the blueprint for the lesson, imagines every possible scenario, and prepares for it.

"First, I storyboarded it."

1. **Long-Range Planning**—The lesson you are planning is only part of a larger plan for the whole year. Make sure you get a picture of the whole calendar year and see how much time you have to carry out what you hope to accomplish. Get a good feel for how each lesson can build off of the previous one and lay the foundation for the next.

2. **Get to Know Your Text and Your Participants**—Get to know your textbook's philosophy, strategies, approaches, strengths, and weaknesses. Get a sense of the whole book and then zero in on a set of chapters or a unit to see how each lesson fits in with the whole. At the same time, get to know the participants in your group. Make adjustments as needed.

3. **Examine the Teacher Notes in the Catechist Manual**—A catechist manual is often a catechist's best friend. Most catechetical texts today have excellent catechist manuals that lay out the lesson much like a blueprint and offer step-by-step instructions. The more you familiarize yourself with the teacher notes, the better you will be able to implement your lesson and still leave room for spontaneity.

4. **Visually Imagine Yourself Teaching the Lesson**—Use your imagination to visualize the lesson you are about to teach. Imagine every possible scenario and your reaction. Picture how much time each segment of your lesson is going to take. Keep a notepad to jot down thoughts or ideas that can now become part of your lesson. Write down a list of materials that you will need for certain situations. Imagine problems that might arise and visualize how you may best handle them. With this visualization complete, you will feel as though you've already taught this lesson once and are now building upon it.

5. **Make Adjustments to Fit the Needs of Your Participants**—No lesson plan is ironclad and unchangeable. Once you've picked up the main focus of the lesson, think of your participants and their unique needs and make any necessary adjustments. You may have participants that are not very talkative, but the lesson calls for discussion. Perhaps you will need to make an adjustment and allow for some nonverbal form of expression. Whatever the case, the better you know your participants, the better you'll be able to make adjustments so that the lesson will be as effective as possible.

6. **Know Your Learning Outcomes (Objectives)**—Know what your participants are supposed to be able to know and/or do as a result of this lesson. Don't settle for the old "my objective is to cover chapter four" routine. Learning outcomes (sometimes referred to as "objectives") are statements found in your lesson plan that state concretely and in measurable terms what it is that your participants should be able to know and do when the session is complete. Without these stated learning outcomes, you would never have any hope of knowing whether you've accomplished what you had set out to do. (For more on learning outcomes, see chapter 8.)

> "He who would climb to a lofty height must go by steps, not leaps."
> —Pope St. Gregory the Great

7. **Follow a Catechetical Process**—Think of your lesson as a movement: you want to move your learners from where they are to where Jesus wants them to be. This movement, called the *catechetical process*, involves four steps:

   1. *Engaging* the life experiences of the participants
   2. *Exploring* the concepts to be taught (Scripture and Tradition)
   3. *Reflecting* and integrating the concepts with the lived experience
   4. *Responding* with a new way of living

   Simply put, you take learners from where they are and move them toward Jesus. St. Ignatius of Loyola described this as entering through their door but leaving through your door.

8. **Get Your Materials Ready**—Be sure that you have all the materials you will need to complete the lesson properly. There's nothing worse than reaching a point in the lesson when you tell participants to cut pictures out of magazines only to find out that you don't have scissors (or magazines). Visualizi ng the lesson ahead of time will help you to see what materials you will need, which perhaps were not listed in the catechist manual.

9. **Have Plan B Ready**—By visualizing the lesson ahead of time, you may discover that what you're hoping to accomplish may not work. Always have an option ready in case something falls flat or just isn't working the way you had hoped.

10. **Overplan**—When serving dinner, it is always better to have more food than not enough. Likewise, when it comes to your lessons, it is always better to prepare more than you think you'll need. Until you learn how to gauge your time effectively, it is quite possible that what you think will comprise an entire session will only cover half of the allotted time. When this happens, panic tends to set in. On the other hand, if you have more material than you need, you can relax and decide how to adjust your next session to make room for what you didn't accomplish in this session.

> As a catechist, ask not what you are going to cover in a lesson, but, rather, what your learners are going to be able to know and do as a result of the lesson.

11. **Pray**—Before you sit down to plan a lesson, take some time to pause and ask the Holy Spirit to guide you. Do your planning and preparation in a prayerful environment. Light a candle. Put on some instrumental music. Place a Bible on the table next to you. Dim the lights. Ask the Holy Spirit to inspire and guide you and to give you the help you need to be focused, loving, and creative.

Glossary

Goals—A goal is a general statement of direction for the lesson. It is a broad statement and is not always measurable. It is a guiding statement for the lesson or unit. (Example: Participants will explore themes in St. Paul's letters.)

Learning Outcomes—A learning outcome is a more concise statement of expected performance or behavior—stated in behavioral terms. (Example: Participants will identify four major components of St. Paul's letters and will compose a contemporary letter using those four components.) Often, the word *objectives* is used interchangeably with the phrase *learning outcomes*.

Catechetical Process—The catechetical process is the practice of transmitting God's word by engaging the lived experience of the learners. This is done by exploring Scripture and Tradition, reflecting upon how God's word and the lived experience are integrated, and responding with a new way of looking at and living life as a follower of Jesus.

Troubleshooting

➕ **If you don't have—and are unable to acquire—a catechist manual, thoroughly read through the participant text and develop your own goals and learning outcomes before writing out a step-by-step plan for your lesson.**

➕ **If your lesson is not working perfectly at first, do not abandon it.** Be patient. Be prepared to switch gears, but don't be too quick to do so.

➕ **If your mind is drawing a blank during your planning and preparation, take a break.** Come back to it later and don't hesitate to ask others for help.

Scripture

"Everyone who listens to these words of mine and acts on them will be like a wise man who built his house on rock. The rain fell, the floods came, and the winds blew and buffeted the house. But it did not collapse; it had been set solidly on rock. And everyone who listens to these words of mine but does not act on them will be like a fool who built his house on sand. The rain fell, the floods came, and the winds blew and buffeted the house. And it collapsed and was completely ruined." (MATTHEW 7:24–27)

Prayer

Lord Jesus, rabbi and teacher, help me to build my lessons upon the solid rock foundation of good planning and preparation. And when the wind comes and the rains buffet, may my teaching withstand the challenges so that those I teach may come to know that your word will endure all things, for you are Lord forever and ever. Amen.

For an opportunity to companion with other catechists and to nourish our vocation, visit www.catechistsjourney.com.

Chapter Three

Socket and Wrench Set: Finding Activities That Fit

I know it's wrong to covet, but I must admit to a vice that I have: I covet certain socket wrench sets—the ones with over 150 different sizes of sockets. Whenever I get the sale ads for the hardware/home improvement megastores, I drool over these shiny collections of sockets. It's amazing how handy these sets can be. When assembling or repairing anything with nuts and bolts, one can encounter a myriad of sizes and shapes. With a vast array of sockets on hand, you can find one that fits perfectly so that you can get the job done.

> "Content and method interact and harmonize in the communication of the faith."
> *National Directory for Catechesis*, 29

Planning Activities That Fit

As part of your planning and preparation, you will ultimately determine an action plan (a format in which your lesson will be experienced). You may find yourself selecting one of the following: lecture, role-play, debate, poster work, group work, discussion, guest speaker, reading the text, or quiz game. How do you know which one to pick? Will the method of activity you choose fit with your learning outcomes? Like finding the right size socket, you need to determine if the activity you have chosen is a good fit both for your lesson and for your particular group of participants. We need to not only alter our activities for variety but also make sure that what we have chosen is the best vehicle for achieving our learning outcomes. It is also important that we modify our activities so that they are appropriate for the particular age group we are teaching.

> You wouldn't rent a car or take a train if your destination was Hawaii! By the same token, you wouldn't have your learners role-playing if the desired outcome was to experience God in the silence of solitude!

Step-by-Step Instructions for Making Sure Your Activities Fit

1. **Review Your Learning Outcomes—** If you know your learning outcomes well, you will have a good idea of the type of activity you should choose. If the learning outcomes call for the participants to express or articulate an understanding of a certain topic, then you know you need to do something other than lecture if you are to accurately assess their ability to express or articulate. If the lesson calls for an understanding of community, it should be obvious to you that some type of group work would be appropriate. Common sense will often dictate which vehicle you must choose.

2. **Review the Age, Gender, and Spiritual Maturity of Your Group—** Visualize your group and imagine yourself delivering the lesson you've planned. Ask yourself if they are capable of being engaged with this approach. Perhaps they are not mature enough. On the other hand, maybe they are more sophisticated than the activity you've chosen.

3. **Consult a List of Possible Learning Activities—** If you have 150 sockets in your tool kit, you'll most likely find one that fits the job at hand. As a catechist, you also have a wide range and variety of activities to select from. Don't get caught in a rut of doing the same thing every time you teach. The next chapter provides a list of various learning activities and discusses what is involved in making them work properly.

4. **Select an Appropriate Activity and See if It Fits—** Once you select an activity to use, add it into your lesson plan and see if it connects with your introduction and conclusion. Ask yourself if this activity will help your learners to achieve the learning outcomes you have set for them. Likewise, ask yourself how this activity will help you to observe and assess those desired outcomes. If you are prepared to go with a particular activity, be sure you are prepared with all of the materials you may need to implement it.

5. **Select an Alternate Activity**—As always, be prepared to switch gears if need be. If your selected activity is failing or just doesn't fit, be prepared with another as a backup. A good example of this is the catechist who is all set to show a video only to discover that the DVD player doesn't work or couldn't be obtained that particular day or time. Always be ready to move on to an alternate plan of action.

Learning activities are not just something for your participants to do—they are accomplishments to be achieved. Learning activities are strategies. When selecting a learning activity, you're not thinking so much about what learners are to do at the *beginning* of the activity but of what they are to accomplish or achieve at the *end* of the activity. Simply put, you tell your learners what you would like for them to accomplish and then give them strategies for doing so.

> Learning activities are not designed to "cover" material but to "uncover" learning!

Glossary

Pedagogy—Refers to the art of teaching, especially in relation to teaching methods. A catechist who has good pedagogy is one who understands the various methods available and utilizes them well.

Methodology—Refers to an orderly arrangement of things. A competent catechist employs the proper methodology, or "orderly arrangement," of the lesson in order to achieve the stated learning outcomes.

Action Plan—Your lesson plan is a lot more than simply "cover chapter five." A catechist needs an action plan, or a step-by-step plan for moving through the lesson, that employs a variety of methods and activities.

Troubleshooting

✚ **If you find yourself in a teaching rut, consult a list of various teaching activities (as found in the next chapter) and try some on for size.** You may be suffering from a simple case of monotony.

✚ **If an activity you have chosen is not working or is inappropriate, examine why.** Look at the age appropriateness of your selection and examine the spiritual and emotional maturity of your participants.

✚ **Employing a variety of activities in your lessons requires more preparation but results in more effective catechesis, a more relaxed catechist, more highly engaged participants, better discipline, and increased spontaneity on your part.**

Scripture

"All these things Jesus spoke to the crowds in parables. He spoke to them only in parables, to fulfill what had been said through the prophet:

> *"I will open my mouth in parables,*
> *I will announce what has lain hidden*
> *from the foundation (of the world)."*

(Matthew 13:34–35)

Prayer

Jesus, sometimes you told stories, other times you performed miracles. Sometimes you spoke for long stretches, other times you said very little. Sometimes you used images and metaphors, other times you spoke quite directly. You seemed to know what was right for the appropriate people at the appropriate time. Help me to choose the best way to bring your word to life for those I teach so that glory may be given to your name. Amen.

For an opportunity to companion with other catechists and to nourish our vocation, visit www.catechistsjourney.com.

Chapter Four

Color Charts: Selecting Learning Activities

One of the more enjoyable things about painting a room is looking over all of the color charts and the countless varieties of colors to choose from. You can select anything from apricot beige to sunlight peach, from rose pink to imperial purple. Of course you can always stick with a basic white, or—if you are slightly adventurous—perhaps off-white. How drab! Today, with the thousands of colors available through computer technology, painting a room can be a real exercise in creative expression.

> "A variety of methods is required in order to ensure that the Gospel is proclaimed to all the nations."
>
> *National Directory for Catechesis, 29*

Learning Activities

All too often, catechists find themselves locked into the same old "color scheme" when it comes to learning activities: there's your basic white (reading from the text) and your off-white (the catechist

speaking about the text). Like imaginative home decorators, we catechists need to realize that there are countless varieties of learning activities available to add color and excitement to any lesson. Like when we use a color chart, we need to look over the possibilities and ask what would be most appropriate. While hot pink may be your favorite color, it may not be the best color to paint your teenage son's bedroom. By the same token, while there are a variety of wonderful activities to choose for your lessons, you need to be sure the activity fits your group and your learning outcomes.

1. **Become thoroughly familiar with the various learning activities available to you**—In the glossary that follows in this chapter, you will find an extensive list of learning activities. Get to know them well before using them.

2. **View these activities in action**—If at all possible, make arrangements to observe another catechist's or Catholic schoolteacher's religion class to see someone use the learning activities that you are interested in implementing.

3. **Review the learning outcomes of your lesson to determine if you have selected the appropriate participant activity for your group.**

4. **Keep all of the materials you need for each particular learning activity well organized and in an accessible place**—This way, when you decide to use that activity, you will have it at your fingertips.

Glossary

Unlike other chapters, this chapter has a glossary that is somewhat extensive. It covers a wide range of learning activities with explanations for how to use them effectively.

Memorizing or "Taking to Heart"—Through catechesis, we sustain the memory of the church. When God gave the Israelites the Ten Commandments, he told them, "Take to heart these words which I enjoin on you today" (Deuteronomy 6:6). While helping your participants take to heart certain doctrinal formulas, you should also inform them of the benefits of the memorization of commonly known prayers of the Christian tradition. When directing your participants to memorize these prayers, which should be appropriate to their age, be sure to help them understand the meaning of what they are taking to heart.

In the ancient world, people believed that the heart—and not the brain—was the seat of the mind and emotions and memories. To this day, when we say that we learn something "by heart," we mean that we are storing it in our mind (memory) and keeping it in a treasured place (emotion).

A catechist decided to have her young class memorize one of the most quoted passages in the Bible: Psalm 23. She gave the youngsters a month to take the verses to heart. Little Ian was excited about the task, but he just couldn't memorize the psalm. After much practice, he could barely get past the first line. On the day that the kids were scheduled to recite Psalm 23 in front of the class, Ian was so nervous. When it was his turn, he stepped up in front of the class and said proudly, "The Lord is my Shepherd, and that's all I need to know."

Speaking and Singing—The spoken or sung word allows participants to not only learn concepts but also to express themselves and articulate and celebrate their faith while growing in the skill of social interaction.

Examples:

- guest speakers
- lectures
- panel discussions
- small-group discussions
- singing (rounds, hymns, Mass parts, nursery rhymes, folk melodies)
- interviews
- large-group discussions
- questions and answers
- storytelling

Once, a mom asked her very young daughter what she learned in religion class. The daughter answered, "We learned that Jesus told us not to be scared and we'll get our quilt." Needless to say, the mom was confused. The next day, she bumped into her daughter's catechist and asked what the lesson was about. The catechist said, "Be not afraid, thy comforter is coming."

Writing—Some people are more comfortable with the written word than with the spoken word. Writing is a powerful vehicle for self-discovery and prayer. Many of the saints used writing to speak with God and with others, and to record their own thoughts. In writing, your participants have an opportunity to clarify their thoughts and to make visible the invisible.

Examples:

- acrostics
- crossword puzzles
- e-mails
- interviews
- letters
- litanies
- logs
- modern parables/stories
- newspaper headlines/stories
- paraphrases
- poems
- prayers
- questions and answers
- quizzes
- raps
- reports
- riddles
- skits
- song lyrics
- speeches
- stories
- slogans
- summaries
- telegrams
- Web pages

A catechist had a very joyful prayer service in the church with his class. Afterward, he asked them to write a letter to God, describing the experience. The following week when the children brought in their letters, one boy wrote, "Dear God, we had a wonderful prayer service in church last week. Wish you could have been there."

Role-Playing and Dramatizing—Through the dramatic stories of our faith, your participants come to understand themselves and others as they internalize the Christian message. Jesus used simple but dramatic stories and parables to invite people to enter into relationship with the Father.

Examples:

- charades
- literature
- choral readings
- dance
- dramatic readings
- gestures to songs
- mime
- pageants
- plays
- puppet shows
- role-playing
- shadow plays
- storytelling

A catechist was preparing her students to dramatize an Old Testament story. She noticed that the boy who was to play the role of Joshua was crying. She asked him what was wrong and he said, "I'm sad for Joshua. He had no parents." The catechist asked him what he was talking about. He replied, "You said that I was to be Joshua, son of Nun."

Playing Games—Young people naturally create and participate in games. Games allow people of all ages to: build community; follow rules; learn about cooperation and participation (as opposed to winning or losing); and develop mentally, physically, and socially. Games encourage the use of problem-solving skills and imagination. The goal of games in catechesis is not simply to have fun but to reinforce or further clarify the focus of your lesson.

Examples:

- bingo
- board games
- card games
- charades
- drawing games
- icebreakers
- mixers
- relays
- skill games
- spelling bees
- team games
- television quiz shows
- tic-tac-toe
- trivia games

Drawing and Art—Faith goes beyond words. Many people express their faith through art and drawing. Your participants can grow spiritually by visually expressing their inner thoughts and feelings. Drawing and art can also help them to become more familiar with religious concepts and relate them to their own lives.

Examples:

- album/CD covers
- banners
- booklets
- bookmarks
- bulletin boards
- bumper stickers
- buttons
- cartoons
- coats of arms
- collages
- comic books
- commemorative stamps
- dioramas
- displays
- doorknob hangers
- finger paintings
- fingerprint pictures from ink pads
- flyers
- greeting cards
- holy cards
- mobiles
- models from clay
- mosaics
- murals
- paper dolls
- paperweights from rocks
- pennants
- photo albums with pictures and captions
- photo essays
- place mats
- plaques
- portraits
- posters
- sculptures
- sidewalk art with chalk
- silhouettes
- sponge paintings
- stained glass
- text lettered on objects (seashells, driftwood, rocks)
- storybooks
- T-shirts
- yarn-and-cloth pictures

"Sorry—He's changed His mind again. Stripes on the zebra, spots on the giraffe, no stars on the lion and make the elephant bigger and the amoebae smaller."

A catechist walked around the room observing what the children were drawing. She asked Erin what she was drawing and the girl responded, "I'm drawing a picture of God." The catechist said, "But nobody knows what God looks like." Erin responded, "They will when I'm done."

Audiovisuals—Although some people think and learn primarily through words, others do so through pictures, images, and sounds. People who are aural/visual learners can develop a deeper appreciation of the message in each lesson when their aural/visual imagination is engaged.

Examples:

- bulletin boards
- CDs, MP3 players, iPods
- chalkboards
- colored chalk
- charts
- computers
- concrete aids
- DVDs
- flannel boards
- LCD projectors
- maps
- models
- movies
- music
- pictures
- PowerPoint presentations
- recordings
- scrapbooks
- slides
- SMART Boards
- transparencies

➕ **If your "color charts" are limited, you need to get bigger, better ones.** If your selection of learning activities is too limited, you need to enlarge it. Do so by slowly acquiring new learning activities. You cannot do this all at once. It takes a great deal of time to acquire a large collection of learning activities. Do it slowly and methodically so as to build your repertoire.

➕ **At the same time, do not lose sight of the fact that sometimes basic white and off-white are all you need.** Often in catechesis, the simple activities of reading a text, leading a simple discussion, or lecturing may actually be the most effective strategy for a particular lesson.

➕ **Finally, if you're not sure about a certain activity, proceed with caution.** You would hate to slap a coat of paint on something that would ruin its true beauty. By the same token, you would hate to use a learning activity that could actually detract from the learning process.

Scripture

"And so it happened. God looked at everything he had made, and he found it very good. Evening came, and morning followed—the sixth day. Thus the heavens and the earth and all their array were completed."

(GENESIS 1:30–2:1)

 Prayer

Lord God, you created this world and its entire array with such beauty and variety. You put the colors of the rainbow in the sky to remind us of your infinite love for us. Help me to participate in your creation by the creative use of variety in my sessions. As you filled the skies with stars, the oceans with swimming creatures, the land with plants and animals of all shapes and sizes, help me to fill my sessions with a variety of learning activities so that the true beauty of your Word will be seen and heard in many colorful ways.

For an opportunity to companion with other catechists and to nourish our vocation, visit www.catechistsjourney.com.

Chapter Five
Different Types of Wood:
Adapting to Learning Styles,
Special Needs, and Diversity

I always thought that wood was wood. Oh, I knew that there were different types, such as maple and oak, but I figured that those names simply identified shades of color. Little did I know that, when it comes to home improvement, different types of wood require different approaches. Some types of wood are classified as soft and others as hard. Some types are suited for furniture, flooring, and paneling, while others are better for making doors, crates, and boxes. The bottom line is that you have to know your different types of wood if you are going to complete effective home improvements.

> "Catechists must be attentive to adapt their method of catechesis to the needs of particular groups they serve."
>
> *National Directory for Catechesis*, 54b-8

Adjusting for Learning Styles

People can be compared to different types of wood. We come in all different varieties, and we can't all be treated in the exact same way. The fact is, people learn in different ways and need to be provided with a variety of learning experiences. In your catechesis, it is important to incorporate approaches that focus on the many learning styles that you will encounter.

1. **Multiple Intelligences**—The concept of multiple intelligences was developed in 1983 by Dr. Howard Gardner, a professor of education at Harvard University. It classifies learners according to their particular strengths. The following listing is adapted from the *Multiple Intelligences SmartCard* (Kagan Publishing and Professional Development):

   a. **Learning through Words**—Some people learn best through activities that focus on words, such as writing, reading, and discussion. It's a good idea to invite these participants to brainstorm ideas, to quiz partners on vocabulary words and the spelling of words, or to summarize the contents of a session in a single word or phrase or by creating a mnemonic device.

   b. **Learning through Music**—A famous song boasts the words, "I've got rhythm." The fact is, some people simply have a good sense of rhythm and melody. To tap into their gift, integrate music into your lessons. Stay current with contemporary music and look for themes and issues in popular songs that are relevant to your lesson. Encourage musical participants to compose lyrics for new or known songs based on the topic you are covering.

   c. **Learning through Logic and Math**—When the bill comes at a restaurant, some people are better than others at figuring out how much everyone owes. In other words, some people are very comfortable with numbers and patterns. To tap into their strength, you can ask participants to connect or relate new learning to previous learning. Invite them to complete surveys related to the theme of your lesson. Likewise, you can create word problems about the material or play questioning games, such as Twenty Questions, which require them to recognize patterns.

   d. **Learning through Art and Space**—People who are more comfortable drawing than writing deserve opportunities to express themselves through art. You can help them by offering opportunities to summarize themes of the lesson by making posters or other displays such as collages, graphs, or charts. Incorporating computer graphics and drawing programs into your lessons will encourage participants to express themselves. In addition, keep in mind the

Catholic church's long history of incorporating sacred art as a form of proclaiming the gospel. Take advantage of opportunities to draw attention to examples of sacred art that help to reinforce the concept you are teaching in your lesson.

> A picture is worth a thousand words. Let your participants draw pictures on occasion. A picture is a lot easier to give feedback on than a thousand-word essay!

e. **Learning through Physical Activity**—Some people simply learn best when they are invited to *do* something. These people, known as *haptic* learners because of their tendency to rely on touch as a primary intake source, are often well coordinated and enjoy using gestures, body language, and hands-on activities. In your lessons, you can use role-playing, athletic activities, simulation exercises, and other content-based games, such as charades and pantomimes, that involve physical movement and tactile activity.

f. **Learning through Nature**—Some people like camping, while others don't. Those who enjoy camping are often keenly aware of the natural world. People such as these tend to learn best when the content of a lesson is related to nature. You can tap into their strength by inviting them to create observation notebooks in which they record various ways of recognizing God's presence in the world around them. Don't hesitate to use microscopes that invite learners to see the complexity of creation. Scavenger hunts are particularly attractive for learners with this gift.

g. **Learning through Interaction**—As members of Christ's church, we enter into community. This is easier for some than for others. Some people learn best by interacting with others. For them, you can provide peer activities, small-group projects and discussions, and large-group activities. You can also develop a pattern for small-group discussions that includes a way to report to the larger group.

h. Learning through Introspection—On the other end of the spectrum are members of Christ's church who are either shy or introspective. They tend to learn best when given time to process information. Provide introspective learners with opportunities to work on their own. You can invite them to keep a reflective notebook in which they can write regularly about what they are learning. Use assessment (see chapter 16) that includes learner portfolios to provide introspective participants an opportunity to express themselves in a way they are most comfortable. Finally, you can incorporate independent learning activities and self-designed study projects into your lessons.

Multiple intelligences can be classified as learning through the following means:

- Words
- Music
- Logic and Math
- Art and Space

- Physical Activity
- Nature
- Interaction
- Introspection

2. **Paying Attention to Special Needs**—You can do much to enhance and emphasize the unity of the Body of Christ by incorporating a positive recognition of the differences in individual abilities. When working with anyone who has special needs, it is important to communicate with your catechetical leader or principal for assistance. Here is an overview of some of the special needs that you may be called upon to integrate into your group, as well as suggestions for helping those with special needs.

a. **Orthopedic Impairment**—You can assist someone who is physically challenged by adapting activities to fit his or her needs. For example, you can develop a buddy system that allows a participant to partner with a physically challenged individual. Prepare in advance for situations in which a physically challenged individual will need assistance. Likewise, make every effort to encourage social interaction. Finally, just as it is important to learn the language of catechesis, it is important to learn and use appropriate terminology when referring to physical disabilities.

b. **Visual Impairment**—To help an individual with visual impairments, consider range of vision as well as lighting needs in relation to where the individual is seated. If possible, provide large-print, audio, and manual materials that can assist the visually impaired. Be conscious of including activities that rely on senses other than sight. Whenever possible, allow a visually impaired learner to work orally and invite another participant to act as his or her partner for activities that are highly visual.

> "When one door closes, another opens. But often we look so long so regretfully upon the closed door that we fail to see the one that has opened for us."
>
> —HELEN KELLER

c. **Deafness or Hearing Impairment**—To assist someone with hearing impairments, arrange for him or her to be seated near the front of the room. Do your best to face the individual when you speak and make every effort to speak clearly, using a normal tone and pace. Write keywords and directions on the board in addition to providing written materials. Again, as in other areas of special needs, encourage social interaction. If needed, arrange for an interpreter—but only in cooperation with the individual's family and your catechetical leader or principal.

d. **Speech or Language Impairment**—In the case of a language barrier, speak clearly and in short phrases. Use visual and written instructions as well as oral instructions. For someone whose oral work needs attention, arrange for an aide to work with him or her in a separate area. In large group settings, allow extra time for a speech-impaired individual to respond to questions and comments.

e. **Social or Behavioral Problems, Attention Disorders, and Learning Disabilities**—Work with the family and your catechetical leader or principal to identify the type of disorder or disability. You can assist by arranging the room to avoid distractions. Provide structure and routine and give, specific tasks that are interesting to the participant. Likewise, be sure to give, review, and clarify directions, expectations, and explanations. Frequently monitor and affirm appropriate behavior, providing immediate feedback. Develop nonverbal clues for unacceptable behavior and break down tasks into smaller, less-overwhelming components. Use flash cards when appropriate and introduce skills one at a time. Rely on visual aids and movement or gestural cues. Finally, request an aide for individualized attention. In all cases, set up situations in which the participant will experience success.

f. **Mental Impairment**—Adapt activities to the participant's attention span and levels of coordination and skill. Individualize learning with the help of an aide, simplify concepts, and repeat your statements periodically. Arrange for a gifted participant to help a slower learner.

g. **Giftedness**—Challenge a gifted participant through independent study, small-group work, enrichment activities, and discovery learning that is related to his or her interest. Strive to provide supplementary resources. Use creative puzzles and games. Ask a gifted individual to help with preparing chapter materials and with assisting slower or younger participants. Encourage high-level thinking skills.

"Really great people make you feel that you, too, can become great."

—Mark Twain

You may need to consider the following special needs in your group:

- ◆ **Orthopedic Impairment**
- ◆ **Visual Impairment**
- ◆ **Deafness or Hearing Impairment**
- ◆ **Speech or Language Impairment**

- ◆ **Social or Behavioral Problems, Attention Disorders,and Learning Disabilities**
- ◆ **Mental Impairment**
- ◆ **Giftedness**

3. **Cultural Inclusivity**—One common mistake made by many well-intentioned catechists in the area of cultural inclusivity is to presume that there is a "norm" (typically Anglo European) that strives to be open and sensitive to others who are not the norm. The fact of the matter is, when it comes to the Body of Christ, there is no norm. As St. Paul said, "There is neither Jew nor Greek, . . . slave nor free . . . , not male and female . . . " (Galatians 3:28). We are all simply members of the Body of Christ. Here are some tips for practicing cultural inclusivity in a consistent manner:

a. Be aware of the diversity in your group and do your "homework" about traditions, customs, and values of the various ethnic groups present in your group.

b. Cultural sensitivity goes beyond race to include awareness that many participants come from families experiencing divorce, mixed-families, various forms of abuse, and lack of attendance at Sunday Mass.

c. Strive to visually reflect the diversity of your group through the display of posters, pictures, and figures of Jesus, the saints, and Bible characters that were created by the cultures of your group.

d. Look at the content of your lessons to see how the lessons might better reflect the diversity in your group.

e. Be aware of various prayer styles and devotions that are customary in certain ethnic groups.

f. Guard against materials, images, and situations that stereotype people of certain ethnic backgrounds. Likewise, avoid qualifiers that reinforce these stereotypes (e.g., identifying someone as "that articulate black man," thus suggesting that he is the exception to the rule).

g. Identify by race or ethnic origin only when relevant. In other words, if it is inappropriate to say, "Cardinal So-and-So, our white archbishop . . . " then it is also inappropriate to say, "Bishop So-and-So, our Hispanic auxiliary bishop . . . ")

h. Be aware of language that, to some people, has questionable racial or ethnic connotations (e.g., survivors of Hurricane Katrina being referred to as "refugees").

"Benjamin, we've discovered, is quite gifted at third base."

i. Be aware of the possible negative implications of color-symbolic words and phrases and ethnic-symbolic words and phrases (e.g., "someone with a black reputation" or "Indian giver").

j. Avoid tokenism toward any racial or ethnic group. In other words, be inclusive on a consistent basis, not just through a once-per-year gesture (e.g., every year, in honor of Martin Luther King Day, we'll take a look at black saints).

> A good catechist is able to: identify weaknesses but emphasize strengths; feel learners' fears but fortify their faith; see their anxieties but free their spirits; and recognize special needs but promote possibilities.

Troubleshooting

A knowledgeable sportscaster once noted that the key to achieving superstardom in any sport is the ability to adjust to an opponent's changing strategies and game plans. Those who do adjust are able to survive, while those who do not adjust struggle and eventually end up in oblivion. Similarly, in order to be a truly effective catechist, you will need to adjust to varying circumstances. Your participants have various learning styles and cultural backgrounds. Also, it is possible that some have special needs. If you simply rely on the same approach no matter who is in front of you, you will ultimately compromise your effectiveness. The more you can do to adjust your style to tap into their strengths, the more effective you will be as a catechist.

Scripture

"To the Jews I became like a Jew to win over Jews; to those under the law I became like one under the law—though I myself am not under the law—to win over those under the law. To those outside the law I became like one outside the law—though I am not outside God's law but within the law of Christ—to win over those outside the law. To the weak I became weak, to win over the weak. I have become all things to all, to save at least some. All this I do for the sake of the gospel, so that I too may have a share in it."

(1 CORINTHIANS 9:20–23)

Prayer

St. Paul taught us that, for the sake of the gospel, we should strive to become "all things to all." Holy Spirit, help me to recognize the wide variety of gifts that are present in the group I teach. Help me to recognize the special needs that some individuals may have and help me to make the necessary adjustments to meet the needs of all my participants. Help me to become all things to all so that I might build up the Body of Christ.

For an opportunity to companion with other catechists and to nourish our vocation, visit www.catechistsjourney.com.

Chapter Six

Drop Cloths: Preparing for Things That Can Go Wrong

When I paint, I often figure that I can accomplish the job with the least amount of effort. Why bother with masking tape, drop cloths, paint thinner, etc., when I can just get started and be done before you know it? You can probably guess the outcome of the times when I've given in to this temptation. I've knocked over paint cans and dropped brushes. I've also gotten paint on the woodwork, on the windows, on the carpet, and on me. I've learned my lesson well. Now, whenever I paint, I painstakingly take a good amount of time to tape around all the edges and place drop cloths everywhere. Furthermore, I keep a supply of paint thinner and a wet rag handy for those unplanned spills. It can be frustrating making all of these preparations. However, in the long run, I have become a much more effective painter. I've learned that what can go wrong *will* go wrong, so why not be prepared?

> "There are . . . many challenges to the ministry of catechesis."
>
> *NATIONAL DIRECTORY FOR CATECHESIS*, 4C

Catechetical Drop Cloths

When you are teaching a lesson, a million and one things can, and often do, go wrong. Whether it is something minor, such as a participant talking out of turn, or a major disruption that brings your lesson to a grinding halt, you need to be prepared in the same way a painter prepares for the many little things that can ruin a job. Let's take a look at the list of what I believe are the top ten things that can and will go wrong in a typical lesson as well as tips for how to deal with and prevent them.

Skills, Tips, and Practical Advice about Things That Can Go Wrong

1. **Your audiovisual equipment either didn't show up or doesn't work—**You don't have to be a technical genius to avoid the problem of audiovisual equipment malfunction. First of all, arrive early to make sure the equipment you need is indeed present. Next, go through a trial run to make sure that: the video, DVD, or CD plays; the volume works; the picture comes on; and the tape/disk is the right one. If something doesn't work the way it is supposed to, you'll have time to correct the problem without an audience watching. We've come to rely heavily on technology in catechesis. However, the success of technology-reliant lessons still lies in the preparedness of the instructor. (For more on the use of technology in catechesis, see chapter 14.)

> **"We've come to rely heavily on technology in catechesis."**

2. **You find yourself short on the amount of handouts/materials needed—**Let's face it, we have so many other things to think about and do that we often don't take time to count how many handouts, books, crayon boxes, or Bibles we have on hand for our lesson. Just as a painter measures the walls to determine how much paint to buy, we need to be very careful and count through all of the supplies and handouts we will use to make sure we have enough. Keep all your materials organized in a briefcase, basket, crate, or bag. A friend of mine always lugs a crate full of teaching supplies around with her and likes to joke about practicing her "PhD"—pulling, hauling, and dragging. The effective catechist knows that adequate supplies are needed, even if it means pulling, hauling, and dragging them along with you!

The Catechist's PhD—
Pull
Haul
Drag

3. **You are emotionally and/or physically run down and can't find the energy needed to teach this lesson**—Completing a task while carrying a burden is very difficult. You may be well prepared and excited about the lesson you are about to teach. Unfortunately, at the last minute you develop a sore throat, your baby spikes a fever of 103, or you and your spouse have an irritating argument about the month's finances right before you leave for lesson. What's a catechist to do? First of all, you and your catechetical leader or principal need to have a contingency plan for arranging a substitute in case of your absence. Likewise, you need to have personal contingency plans in case you need a baby-sitter or other personal arrangements made so that you can teach your lesson. Be aware of the burden you are carrying, but do not under any circumstances attempt to take it out on your participants or seek solace from them. At times like this, you need to pray for the inspiration to acknowledge your burden. Then, set it aside so that the needs of your participants can come first.

> **"Half this game is ninety percent mental."**
> —Yogi Berra

4. **Your participants totally misunderstand the complex directions you thought you just explained, and everything is up for grabs**—To avoid this problem, follow these rules. First, never put participants into a group until *after* you've explained the directions for group work. Second, always *repeat* your directions. Third, ask a participant to repeat the directions back to you so that you can test class comprehension. Finally, continue to repeat the directions—even after the group work or task has begun—so that they are regularly reinforced. Again, this may seem painstaking, but the alternative is chaos or anarchy: take your pick.

> Whatever the case, don't panic. You never signed on to be the fount of all knowledge. By telling the participants that you need to research and learn the answer to the question, you model for them what it means to be a disciple of Jesus.

5. **A participant stumps you with a question that you have no idea how to answer**—You know the type of question: "Did Judas go to hell?" or "Why can't women be priests?" or "If we're eating the Body and Blood of Jesus at communion, doesn't that make us cannibals?" Ouch. These questions can send a catechist into a panic. Here's what you need to do. First, if the question is clearly out of line, politely tell the participant to hold on to that question until another, more appropriate, time. Second, if you think the question is reasonable but you are still stumped, tell the participant that he or she has asked a good question and that you do not know the answer but will find out for the next lesson. Finally, if you're working with older participants, you may invite someone else to answer the question—if they think they know the answer, and you think they are capable of doing so. Whatever the case, don't panic. You never signed on to be the font of all knowledge. By telling the participants that you need to research and learn the answer to the question, you model for them what it means to be a disciple of Jesus.

6. **The lesson, video, or text turns out to be a lemon**—Sorry, but if you find yourself in this mess, it means you haven't done your homework. The only way a catechist can be in the middle of a lesson, video, or text passage that is comprised of poor material is if he or she did not preview the materials. Be sure to read over the text to confirm that it is age appropriate, interesting, and pertinent. Prior to the class, walk through the lesson in your mind to determine if it will work. Furthermore, always watch a video before you show it to your group. We often tend to relax when we show a video, thinking that we have less work to do. On the contrary, showing a video means that you need to take the time to preview its contents, plan a discussion, and get there early to test the AV equipment. The bottom line is: prepare.

7. A minor discipline problem makes you lose your train of thought—You know the kind of minor problems we're talking about: giggling, side talking, tapping a pen, a well-timed burp (or other gastro-intestinal sound effect), etc. Your challenge is to confront the behavior without stopping the lesson. If someone's attention is wavering, call on him or her to get that participant back into the mix. If someone is making noises that are disruptive while you or someone else is talking, go over and stand by that participant. If necessary, place a hand on his or her desk or table-top to make that participant aware of your presence. Don't be a stationary catechist—get up and move around the room. Your proximity to participants is the strongest deterrent against disruptive behavior. Moving around allows you to continue the lesson while relying on eye contact, proximity, or a tap on the shoulder to challenge disruptive behavior. (For more information on dealing with disruptive behaviors, see chapter 10.)

> "I have not failed.
> I've just found 10,000 ways that won't work."
> —THOMAS ALVA EDISON

8. **An interruption (someone at the door) allows the participants just the sliver of opportunity they needed to create a disruption**—It doesn't take much for participants, especially children, to get off track. As a catechist, you basically need to grow eyes in the back of your head. In other words, never turn your back on your group. If you are helping an individual participant, do so in a way that allows you to continue observing the rest of the group. If someone comes to the door, speak to that person while facing your group. Finally, *never* leave your room unattended. Not only do you risk discipline problems, you are also in jeopardy of facing legal concerns.

9. **Someone (a guest speaker or participant doing a presentation) doesn't show up when he or she is supposed to**—You've got it all planned out. The participants will do presentations of the posters they've worked on for your next lesson. The only problem is, three of the five participants scheduled to present their posters that day turn out to be absent because of the chicken pox going around the parish. Once again, you're left holding the bag. This problem may be unavoidable, but you need to have a contingency plan. Always have Plan B ready in case Plan A fails. It need not be elaborate, but you should have some type of activity or lesson ready in case the people you were counting on don't show up.

> You've got it all planned out

10. **You're done with your lesson, and you still have thirty-five minutes to go**—This is every catechist's nightmare. You picture yourself engaged in a great discussion with participants for twenty minutes or so. But then you find out that they are uttering little more than a grunt here and a groan there, and you've completed all your discussion questions in the first five minutes. The key to coping with this problem is to always *overplan*.

> " When you get to your wit's end, you'll find God lives there. "
> —Unknown

Especially as a new catechist, you need to prepare for more than you think can be accomplished in your allotted time. As you become more seasoned, you will develop a better feel for how long a lesson will take and how much material you need. As you overplan, however, don't bite off more than you can chew. It's just as bad to reach the end of the class period only to find out that you need five more minutes to bring closure to your experience. The key to overplanning is to be sure you have extra material that is not necessarily crucial to your lesson. If you need to rely on it, that's fine. If you don't get to it, that's fine too. But don't leave home without it.

> "I find that the harder I work, the more luck I seem to have."
> —Thomas Jefferson

Glossary

Only two words are necessary to understand this chapter on things that can go wrong: *organization* and *preparation*. These words are self-explanatory. If you devote the proper amount of time *preparing* for your lesson and *organizing* your materials, you will either avoid or effectively cope with most anything that can go wrong.

Troubleshooting

⊕ **Don't be alarmed by all the things that can go wrong in your lesson.** This chapter's list of things that can and will go wrong is not intended to frighten you. Quite the contrary, if you are well aware of all the things that can go wrong and how to deal with them, you will be able to deal with them much more effectively. Painters don't get frightened by the possibility of spilling paint—they just bring drop cloths.

⊕ **Having said that, despite being eminently prepared and organized, you may still have things go wrong.** The key to anything that comes up in your lesson is: *don't panic.* If you remain calm and keep your perspective, you will be able to handle almost any problem that comes up.

Scripture

"Which of you wishing to construct a tower does not first sit down and calculate the cost to see if there is enough for its completion? Otherwise, after laying the foundation and finding himself unable to finish the work the onlookers should laugh at him and say, 'This one began to build but did not have the resources to finish.'"

(LUKE 14:28–30)

Prayer

Lord Jesus, sometimes people had a hard time accepting plan. When you spoke in your hometown synagogue, they tossed you out. When you tried to meet the minds of the Pharisees, they responded by trying to trick you. When you taught parables to your disciples, they often did not understand. Yet, you continued to find ways to reach people, even if it meant making a point by washing your disciples' feet. Help me to be prepared for the unexpected in my lessons and to find creative ways to overcome all those little things that can and will go wrong.

For an opportunity to companion with other catechists and to nourish our vocation, visit www.catechistsjourney.com.

Chapter Seven

Applying Primer: Preparing the Learning Environment

"Catechists are to identify and create suitable conditions which are necessary for the Christian message to be sought, accepted, and more profoundly investigated."

National Directory for Catechesis, 54B–8

Before you apply paint or wallpaper to a wall, you have to make sure that you've scraped, filled, sanded, and cleaned the wall. If you're painting, the most important thing you need to do is apply a primer. Only after these things are completed are you ready to apply the paint or wallpaper that will truly bring out the beauty of the room. If you skip all these steps, you will have a finished product that is either seriously flawed or may not work at all. How you prepare the surface is the most important step in completing your painting or wallpapering project.

Preparing Your Teaching Environment

The same wisdom holds true for teaching a lesson as it does for painting a wall. You need to complete some preliminary steps to prepare the environment you will be working in, lest your lesson turn out seriously flawed or fail altogether. Preparing a learning space for a lesson is not unnecessary fluff or fussiness. It is a way of increasing the effectiveness of your lesson, thus allowing you to tap into the true inner beauty of your participants. Jesus gave us good examples. When he taught the Beatitudes—a new law of love—it was no accident that he taught from atop a mount, creating an image of a "new Moses." For the

Last Supper, he took great pains to have preparations made for the room in which the Passover meal would be celebrated. When he multiplied the loaves and fish, he made detailed arrangements to have the five thousand people gathered into groups of fifty or a hundred. If we are to teach as Jesus did, we, too, must pay attention to our environment and make the necessary preparations to increase the effectiveness of our lessons.

Skills, Tips, and Practical Advice for Preparing the Learning Environment

If you were having people over for dinner, you would no doubt prepare the environment to heighten the enjoyment and express a mood of celebration and hospitality. When we teach, we are hosting a "meal" for our participants. We are bringing them nourishment for the spirit and soul. Therefore, we need to take the necessary steps to "set the table."

> When your learners arrive, it should look as though you were expecting them!

1. **Make a Clean, Neat Space**—A job seems twice as overwhelming if it is surrounded by a mess. The same is true of teaching. It is imperative that you and the participants are entering a learning space that is clean, neat, and in order. You want your participants to know that the "food" you will be serving is of the highest quality. If participants see a mess upon entering a room, they will be more than happy to add to it. Likewise, a messy learning space is conducive to messy behavior (i.e., poor discipline). Be sure to arrive early to clean up whatever mess was left from the previous group that used the room.

2. **Provide a Welcoming Seating Arrangement**—Do you recall that when Jesus fed the five thousand, he arranged them into groups of fifty and a hundred? Arranging your "crowd" is crucial to your lesson as well. If at all possible, arrange the desks in a circle or semicircle or some other arrangement that encourages interaction and is also conducive to prayer. Your goal should be to create an arrangement that keeps order but also communicates a sense of welcome, comfort, and community. It should encourage participation while removing intimidation and rigidity.

3. **Provide Name Tags**—Calling your participants by name is a way of honoring them and letting them know that you really are interested in them. It is also a way of keeping order in your room. If a participant is misbehaving, it helps to be able to call him or her by name rather than saying "Hey, you!" In baptism, we were each given a name that is inscribed in heaven. Jesus calls us each by name. We should do no less for our participants. Providing name tags, especially for the first few meetings, is an effective strategy.

4. **Create a Prayer Center**—What is the central focus of your learning environment? Is it a desk or a podium? The chalkboard? In a catechetical setting, it is imperative that the central focus of your space be *Jesus*. You can do this through the prominent placing of a Bible, a candle, and/or a bowl of holy water and a crucifix. If you truly are encouraging your participants to make Jesus the center of their lives, begin by making Jesus the center of your learning space.

> In a catechetical setting, it is imperative that the central focus of your space be *Jesus*.

Visuals serve to reinforce the sacramental nature of the Catholic faith. We recognize God in all things. Posters, pictures, and sacred objects can be channels of God's grace for your participants.

5. **Display Posters, Pictures, and Sacred Objects**—We live in a very visual age. By the time participants reach your learning space, they have been conditioned to receive more information visually than aurally. Take advantage of this fact by putting up posters and religious images that can reinforce your lesson. Pictures and posters of Scripture stories and the saints can make for an effective addition to your lesson. Sacred objects and images can also add to the message you are teaching. Likewise, photos of your participants in action can show just how much importance you really place on them. If you're sharing the space with another group, you can easily create a portable display panel (using a trifold display board) that you can carry in and out for your lesson and use as a focal point.

6. **Utilize the Chalkboard, Easel, Wipe-Off Board, and Overhead Projector**—Arrive early and write key phrases, directions, or names and definitions on the board, easel, or overhead. This way, when your lesson begins, you can refer to these images without turning your back on your participants to write. This gives the participants the strong message that you are prepared and that there *is* work to be done. For those more technologically advanced, a SMART Board connected to a notebook computer is also available, as is an LCD projector for doing a PowerPoint presentation. (For more information, see chapter 14.)

7. **Organize a Supply Station**—After Jesus fed the five thousand, he instructed the disciples to gather all the leftovers into baskets. Jesus knew that the key to making the most of resources was to be organized. Be sure to have a supply station to keep all supplies—such as handouts, textbooks, pencils, crayons, glue, and scissors—well organized and at your fingertips. Whether it is a table, a desk, a shelf, a cabinet, or a crate, you need to have your supplies organized. By doing so, you do not need to interrupt your lesson to go in search of them when they are needed. Again, if you are sharing your learning space with others, a portable supply station can do the trick.

8. **Use Technology**—Jesus didn't use VCRs or CD/DVD players. He did, however, use the medium of his time—he taught using parables. We, too, must take advantage of the medium of our time. The proper use of technology can greatly enhance a lesson. You do not have to be a technical genius to handle this equipment either. If you are showing a video or DVD, or playing a tape or CD, be sure you've got it set to start at the right place. (For more information on using technology in catechesis, see chapter 14.)

9. **Straighten Up before Leaving**—As your session is coming to an end, have the participants straighten the room. They should be responsible for: gathering up materials and textbooks; repositioning tables, chairs, and desks; and displaying their work on bulletin boards or posters. By displaying their work, they are able to see the progress they are making. Like a decorator standing back to see how nice the wallpapering is coming along, you and your participants also need to stand back and admire what can be done with God-given talents.

Prayer Center—A small table in the center of a room with a Bible, a candle, and/or a bowl of holy water and a crucifix placed there as a visual focus for the participants.

Functionality—A learning space must be designed to serve the participants and the catechist as well as the goals of the lesson. While aesthetics are important, the bottom line is whether the design will work for the learning activity.

> " Success depends upon previous preparation, and without such preparation there is sure to be failure. "
> —Confucius

Troubleshooting

⊕ **If you do not have a learning space to call your own, or if you share it with another catechist or schoolteacher, you will need to think "portable."** Bring along whatever you need to prepare the space for your lesson. You will also need to arrive especially early so that you can make your arrangements.

⊕ **If you have stationary desks or are asked to not move the ones in your learning space, your hands are tied to some extent.** However, you may be able to have your participants (especially children and teens) sit on the floor if space allows. Speak to your catechetical leader or principal about occasionally moving to an open space like a school hall, chapel, auditorium, or even outdoors (weather permitting). You may wish to place more emphasis on activities that get participants out of their desks.

⊕ **If you are in a home teaching environment, you are not off the hook.** In fact, you may need to pay even more attention to these preparations so that usual home distractions (TV, music, view of neighbors' kids playing, etc.) don't interfere. Portable display panels and a prayer center can be very effective in a home setting.

- **If you lack the financial resources to prepare your learning space, you need to use your imagination.** Several pieces of poster paper taped to the wall can serve as an effective "chalkboard." Your own Bible and a small vigil candle can create a nice prayer center. Holy water is free. Have the participants create posters to decorate the learning space. Name "tents" can be made from index cards and placed in front of each participant to replace the use of expensive name tags. In other words, meager financial resources simply mean that your own creative resources will need to be called upon even more.

- **Again, don't panic if you are unable to accomplish some of the things discussed in this chapter.** They are meant to enhance the lesson. If Peter and the apostles were able to teach the first lessons of Christianity on the street corners of Jerusalem, we, too, can find ways of teaching our lessons, no matter where we find ourselves.

"We bring gold and frankincense. The myrrh is in the mail."

"'Wherever he enters, say to the master of the house, "The Teacher says, 'Where is my guest room where I may eat the Passover with my disciples?'" Then he will show you a large upper room furnished and ready. Make the preparations for us there.' The disciples then went off, entered the city, and found it just as he had told them; and they prepared the Passover."

(MARK 14:14–16)

Prayer

Jesus, before you gathered with your disciples for the Passover, you made sure all of the proper preparations were taken care of. You knew that the space you were gathering in was important for what you were about to do. Help me to make the arrangements I need in my learning space to make my lessons more effective and to bring order and life to my lessons. May I pay great attention to the details of my lessons so that they may be as effective as possible.

For an opportunity to companion with other catechists and to nourish our vocation, visit www.catechistsjourney.com.

Chapter Eight

Spotlights: Shifting the Focus onto Learners

It seems that repairs of important circuits, pipes, wires, and conduits in our homes often need to be done in the darkest, dingiest corners of the attic or basement. Getting to them is never easy. Seeing them is even harder. Without my trusty spotlight, I would never be able to change a fuse or reconnect a loose wire in one of those dark corners. There are whole corners of the crawl space, attic, or basement

> "The active participation of all the catechized in their Christian formation fosters learning by doing."
>
> *NATIONAL DIRECTORY FOR CATECHESIS*, 29G

that were previously completely in the dark but now come to life under the bright beam of the spotlight. A funny thing happens, however, when I work with a spotlight. Eventually, somehow, it gets turned and twisted until it is no longer shining on what I need to see but is shining right into my eyes. Needless to say, this is uncomfortable. More importantly, it is detrimental to what I'm trying to accomplish. The spotlight is not supposed to be on me but on my repairs.

Putting the Focus on Your Participants and Away from Yourself

When I was a student teacher, I was very proud of the first class I taught. My mouth had a motor on it, and I never ran out of gas. When class was over, my cooperating teacher congratulated me on surviving and said that I did a good job. Then, he bluntly said, "You talk too much." I said, "I thought teachers were supposed to talk." "Yes," he replied, "but not all the time. The spotlight is not supposed to be on you, it's supposed to be on your students. They are the ones who are supposed to perform, not you." This was a "Copernican revolution" for me, but it made great sense. If I do all the performing, then I become an entertainer, and the participants become a passive audience. The spotlight is shining in the wrong place.

In every learning space, there is a spotlight waiting to shine. If we focus that light totally on ourselves, we are putting a great deal of pressure on ourselves. Our goal as catechists is to turn that spotlight around and shine it on the entire group of participants. We need to learn how to shift the focus or pressure off ourselves and onto the group, where it will allow us to see our participants in a whole new way.

Skills, Tips, and Practical Advice for Shifting the Focus onto Learners

Catechists tend to put a lot of pressure on themselves to do all the talking. This is a hard habit to break. Here are some tips on how to shift the focus away from yourself and onto your participants:

1. **Look over Your Lesson Plan**—How much talking are *you* planning on doing? Sometimes lecture is necessary; but if you are always doing all of the talking, when and how will the participants learn to express their faith? Use some of your talking time to brainstorm ways of getting the participants involved in bringing forth the material you wish to cover.

2. **Review Your Learning Outcomes**—Remember, your learning outcomes are not statements about what *you* are going to do, but descriptions of what your *participants* are going to do. If your outcomes call for participants to articulate an understanding of the Beatitudes, then that means that *they* are to articulate that understanding—not you. Most catechetical textbooks articulate the learning outcomes for a lesson. As you grow in your role as a catechist, you will learn to develop your own learning outcomes when needed. The key to learning outcomes is that they must be measurable: they must identify a behavior or skill that you will be able to look for (assess). The following is a convenient chart that provides some keywords for measurable learning outcomes.

If you want your participants to . . .	Use keywords such as the following in your learning outcomes:		Example: *After this lesson, the participants will be able to . . .*
recognize or recall facts, information, and knowledge (recall)	list define fill in name	describe repeat label identify	list the seven sacraments.
demonstrate an understanding (comprehension)	paraphrase review discuss	explain match interpret	explain the meaning of the symbol of water in baptism.
apply what is learned to new situations (application)	apply draw sketch write	construct simulate predict	draw a picture of an experience of reconciliation in their lives.
pick out important points (analysis)	classify differentiate contrast separate	distinguish compare categorize break down	categorize the seven sacraments into Sacraments of Initiation, Sacraments of Healing, and Sacraments at the Service of Communion.
combine concepts into something new (synthesis)	combine put together assemble	relate integrate collect	assemble a prayer aid for the celebration of one of the seven sacraments.
judge and evaluate ideas based on standards (evaluation)	judge assess decide rate evaluate	argue appraise defend debate choose	evaluate a sample homily for a confirmation Mass in relation to its use of the gifts of the Holy Spirit, the symbols of the bishop, or the symbols of the rite of confirmation.

3. **Identify Ways in Which Participants Will Be Engaged in Learning**—Participants can demonstrate learning and understanding in a wide variety of ways (many are discussed in chapter 3). Don't rely solely on oral expression. Provide your participants with a variety of ways (drawing, writing, role-playing, poster making, etc.) in which they can demonstrate an understanding of material. The old image of learners as sponges who will soak up the information you offer them does not work. They are already saturated with information that society bombards them with and will not be able to retain what you offer them. However, experts estimate that learners retain 90 percent of what they *do*. Get your learners *doing*.

> Experts estimate that learners retain 90 percent of what they *do*. Get your learners *doing*.

4. **Be Prepared with Open-Ended Questions**—Strive to use questions that are "open-ended" or, simply put, those that cannot be answered with a yes or a no. For example, instead of asking, "Do you remember your first communion?" ask, "What are some of the things you remember about your first communion?" Granted, you may still get one-word answers, but if you have more than yes or no, you can at least begin making a list on the board for further discussion. (For more information about techniques for asking questions, see chapter 15.)

5. **Develop Techniques for "Deflecting"**—Difficult questions can put the heat of the spotlight right on you. Learn to deflect such questions by shifting the attention off of yourself and onto the question. Respond to a difficult question by tossing it back at the questioner ("What do *you* think?") or by inviting anyone else in the group to share their thoughts while you compose yourself and collect your

A catechist began her lesson with a question. "Boys and girls, what do we know about God?"

A hand shot up in the air. "He is an artist!" said a young boy.

"Really?! How do you know?" the catechist asked.

"You know—'Our Father, who does art in heaven . . .'"

own thoughts. Jesus was very good at this. He often responded to a question with a question. For example, when the Pharisees asked Jesus where he gets the authority to forgive sins, Jesus replied by asking, "Where was John's baptism from? Was it of heavenly or of human origin?" (Matthew 21:25).

6. **Resist the Temptation to Talk Too Much**—I imagine it would have been easier for Jesus if he had given a lecture to his disciples about who he was. Instead, he asked them two questions: "Who do people say that I am?" and "Who do *you* say that I am?" (Mark 8:27, 29; emphasis added). Jesus did not jump in with the correct answer but waited for the disciples to offer the best replies they could. As catechists, we, too, need to resist the temptation to give the answers and help our participants grapple with the questions of life and faith.

> **"**Practice is the best of all instructors **"**
> —PUBLILIUS SYRUS

Glossary

Focus—This is another word for the "spotlight," or a way of determining who the attention is on. On TV, a good interviewer keeps the focus not on him-or herself but on the guest. As a catechist, you need to be sure the focus or attention is not always on you but on the participants and the subject matter.

"I don't have an answer, but you've sure given me a lot to think about."

➕ **If you feel the pressure mounting while you are teaching, think of the spotlight metaphor.** When you feel too much pressure, chances are there is too much focus on you. Don't panic. Gradually shift the focus onto the group and away from yourself.

➕ **Remind yourself that you are not there to perform but to make sure that the participants do.** By the same token, get used to the spotlight. Stage fright is natural, and you will learn to overcome it.

➕ **If you feel uncomfortable under the spotlight, you can bet the participants will, too.** Show by example that it is OK to have the focus on you for a while.

Scripture

"Nothing is concealed that will not be revealed, nor secret that will not be known. What I say to you in the darkness, speak in the light; what you hear whispered, proclaim on the housetops."

(MATTHEW 10: 26–27)

Prayer

Jesus, I believe that you have spoken to my participants in the dark, mysterious corners of their hearts. Help me to shine the light on them so that they will bring out what is concealed and make known what is hidden. Give me the courage and strength I need to resist the temptation to talk all the time. Help me put the focus on my participants so that they will come to realize that the real light comes from within.

For an opportunity to companion with other catechists and to nourish our vocation, visit www.catechistsjourney.com.

Chapter Nine

Extension Cords: Plugging into the Power of Prayer

I was all set to begin paneling my basement. I had all the panels and nails ready, as well as my electric drill and all of my drill bits. I put the drill into place to get started, pressed the power button, and—nothing. I wasn't plugged in. I looked around and noticed that the nearest outlet was all the way over on the other side of the room. Did I have an extension cord? Take a guess. It's frustrating when you have all the tools ready to complete a project, but you're missing the one thing that will get you going: the power to make it all happen.

> "Because catechesis seeks to lead persons and communities to deeper faith, it is oriented to prayer and worship."
>
> *NATIONAL DIRECTORY FOR CATECHESIS*, 34

The Power of Prayer

As a catechist, you may have all the tools needed to complete your lessons. Yet without prayer, it's like trying to drill holes without an extension cord: if you're not plugged in, forget it. Personally, you need prayer to sustain yourself and your own level of creativity and commitment. Your participants need prayer because without a personal affective relationship with God in their lives all the doctrine in the world can seem meaningless.

In a good lesson, prayer is not just the frosting on the cake. It is not just a set of bookends to open and close a session. Prayer is the "yeast" that makes the "dough" of our lessons come to life. Prayer is the extension cord we need in order to reach out to and plug into our source of energy: our Creator, God. Prayer *is* part of the content and doctrine of our lessons. As we pray, so we believe. As we believe, so we pray. To teach prayer is to teach a way of life.

> Your participants need prayer because without a personal affective relationship with God in their lives, all the doctrine in the world can seem meaningless.

Because the *General Directory for Catechesis* teaches us that the most effective catechesis takes place within a climate of prayer, we will devote more space to this topic than to most chapters in this book.

Leading Others in Prayer

Praying with others can be an intimidating experience for some of us. As you mentor your participants to pray, you guide them to know that they can strengthen their personal relationship with God by praying almost anywhere.

Skills, Tips, and Practical Advice for Leading Others in Prayer

1. **Preparing a Prayer Center**—Invite your participants to help you create this sacred space. A prayer center can be a simple table draped with a cloth to show the liturgical season. On the table you can place a Bible, along with a crucifix, a statue, an icon, or another religious object. Creating this space demonstrates the value of prayer and builds an awareness of the sacred. If space permits, use it as a place for all to gather around for prayer.

2. **Enthroning the Bible**—We show reverence for God's word by "enthroning" the Bible—respectfully placing it in an open position in the prayer center. Invite participants to participate in a procession (especially when working with children) led by a volunteer holding the closed Bible high while the others follow singing a song or an alleluia. Another participant may receive the Bible, open it, and reverently place it in the prayer center for all to see.

3. **Taking Traditional Prayers to Heart: Memorization and Prayer**—One of the ways that we sustain the "memory" of the church is through the memorization, or "taking to heart," of traditional prayers. Traditional prayers are like family heirlooms—they have been passed on from generation to generation. These prayers link your participants to basic truths of our faith by supporting personal prayer and allowing groups of people to unite their minds, hearts, and voices in prayer. Be sure that your participants understand the meaning of the words in the prayers they are taking to heart.

> Traditional prayers are like family heirlooms—they have been passed on from generation to generation.

4. **Lectio Divina**—Lectio divina, Latin for "sacred reading," is a way of spending time with the word of God using a special form of reading and listening so that we can hear God "with the ear of our hearts" (St. Benedict, Prologue to the Rule). In our hectic world, this quiet and contemplative form of prayer is a welcome transformation. This form of prayer follows four steps.

   a. **Lectio** (reading)—Slowly and prayerfully read aloud a brief Scripture passage, repeating the passage up to three times after a silent pause between each reading. Listeners are encouraged to allow a word or phrase to speak to them in a special way. After one of the readings of the passage, participants may be invited to share (without trying to explain) the word or phrase that is speaking to them.

   b. **Meditatio** (meditation)—The listeners silently reflect for a few minutes upon the word or phrase that is speaking to them. In doing so, participants take the word or phrase to heart and allow it to interact with their own thoughts, hopes, desires, and memories.

   c. **Oratio** (prayer)—The participants now enter into a silent dialogue with God for a few minutes, speaking as one friend speaks to another and allowing themselves to be touched and changed by God's word.

d. Contemplatio (contemplation)—The participants simply rest silently and prayerfully in God's embrace for a few minutes. By letting go of their own words, participants allow the word of God to speak to their hearts in silence.

5. **Leading Reflective Prayer (Meditation)**—As we share reflective prayer or meditation, we lead participants to use reflection and imagination, to engage in prayerful conversation with God, and to recognize his presence in their daily lives. Here are some basic steps for leading reflective prayer.

a. **Getting Ready for Reflective Prayer**—Invite the participants to focus on God's presence. Establish a quiet, prayerful, and comfortable environment and mood to help them overcome distractions. This first step may take anywhere from three to five minutes. Consider the following as you join them in reflective prayer:

   (1) **Encourage a Comfortable Posture**—If possible, move your participants to the prayer center and invite them to find a position in which they can be comfortable yet alert. If space is limited, invite them to get comfortable in their seats. Encourage your participants to close their eyes or to focus their attention on a symbol or a picture.

   (2) **Invite Deep Breathing**—Take two or three minutes to help the participants to relax and breathe deeply. Ask them to rest their hands and to slowly and silently breathe in deeply and then breathe out gradually. Help them establish a rhythm to their breathing by having them count slowly to three as they breathe in, and asking them to breathe out as you count to three.

   (3) **Use Reflective Music**—Reflective (instrumental) music can help by covering distractions and providing a soothing setting.

b. **Leading the Reflective Prayer**—Begin the reflective prayer with an invitation to reflect or meditate on an aspect of the theme that you are teaching—often a Scripture passage or a traditional prayer. Reflection time with your participants can range from just a few minutes to a half hour, depending on the age of your group and the circumstances.

(1) Step-by-Step Directions— Through a series of age-appropriate "directions" that you have prepared or are following from a resource (such as a book of guided meditations for children, teens, or adults), you invite your participants to engage their imagination and enter into a setting where they can encounter Jesus, dwell on his words, and converse with him. (For an example of a guided reflection, see Appendix 1.)

> Reflective prayer uses an approach inspired by St. Ignatius of Loyola. It invites us to pray by using the senses of imagination—sight, hearing, smell, taste, and touch.

(2) Speaking Slowly and Pausing—By speaking slowly and pausing for emphasis after each line of the reflection, you invite the participants to pray more reflectively.

(3) Engaging Imagination—Reflective prayer uses an approach inspired by St. Ignatius of Loyola. It invites us to pray by using the senses of imagination—sight, hearing, smell, taste, and touch. We thereby create a setting in our minds: a welcoming place—whether it is a biblical setting or a place of our own choice—to enter into conversation with Jesus. St. Ignatius said that such conversation should resemble the way "one friend speaks to another" (*The Spiritual Exercises of Saint Ignatius*, 54).

Johnny had been misbehaving, and the catechist asked him to put his head down and pray for a few minutes. After a while, he lifted his head and told his catechist that he had thought it over and had then said a prayer.

"Fine," said the pleased catechist. "If you ask God to help you not misbehave, He will help you."

"Oh, I didn't ask Him to help me not misbehave," said Johnny. "I asked Him to help you put up with me."

c. **Allowing Quiet Time with God**—In closing, invite the participants to spend time in silence with God, while being aware of God's presence. This is called contemplation. This last step may take anywhere from three to five minutes.

(1) **Silent Prayer**—Invite your participants to rest in God's presence. Allow one or two minutes for silent prayer, depending on the responsiveness of the group.

(2) **Transition**—A few gentle words provide a gradual transition, inviting the participants into the next activity.

(3) **Respect**—Your participants' thoughts and reflections in prayer are theirs alone. You show respect for their conversation with God by letting them keep these thoughts to themselves.

6. **Leading Liturgical Prayer**—A more structured or formal prayer experience, often referred to as a prayer service, is a form of *liturgical prayer*. This means that it is a shared communal prayer with assigned roles (such as leader, reader, group 1, group 2, left, right, etc.) and a specific order (song, greeting, opening prayer, Scripture reading, etc.). Here are some things to keep in mind when planning and leading liturgical prayer.

a. **Ask Yourself, "What Is the Assembly Doing?"**—When planning liturgical prayer, it can often be tempting to focus on what you, as the prayer leader, are doing

> Be sure that a prayer service is not something that is done by just a few but is truly a liturgical experience: the work of all who are gathered.

throughout the prayer. Be sure to ask yourself, "What is the assembly doing?" throughout the prayer. This does not mean that every participant must have an individual role, but that the assembly as a whole is participating actively in the prayer through singing, responding, listening, praying in silence, sharing traditional prayers, taking part in ritual action, and so forth. Be sure that a prayer service is not something that is done by just a few but is truly a liturgical experience: the work of all who are gathered.

b. **Assign Roles ahead of Time**—Before beginning a liturgical prayer, be sure that everyone knows his or her assigned part. Readers should have an opportunity to prepare their parts ahead of time. If there are parts to be prayed aloud that you've assigned to "left" and "right" or group 1 and group 2, be sure to tell your participants ahead of time which side or group they belong to. If there is a ritual gesture that needs explaining (e.g., participants coming forward to bless themselves with holy water), give directions ahead of time so that the prayer can flow smoothly.

c. **Consider the Following "Ingredients"**—Liturgical prayer follows a definite, though not a rigid, order. As you plan a prayer service, consider including the following ingredients or elements:

(1) **Song**—Singing and music are not just the background noise of a prayer service. St. Augustine taught, "To sing once is to pray twice." Singing is a way of raising our minds and hearts to God by raising our voices. It is also a way of gathering our minds and hearts into a community of faith as our voices become one. Finally, liturgical song is also catechetical: the

"I'm sorry, Mr. Landis, would you repeat the question? I was lost in prayer."

Extension Cords: Plugging into the Power of Prayer

lyrics to our hymns teach about our faith. A traditional Latin phrase says *Lex orandi, lex credendi,* which means "the law of prayer is the law of faith." This means that we pray (including singing) according to our beliefs.

(2) Silence—Resist the temptation to fill every space of a prayer service with words and sounds. Silence is a crucial form of prayer. Many contemplatives consider silence to be the primary language of God. Allow for silence at various points throughout a prayer service, especially after Scripture is proclaimed. Brief directions for what to focus on during periods of silence can be helpful.

Silence is a crucial form of prayer

(3) The Sign of the Cross—As mentioned earlier, Catholics pray sacramentally. Beginning our prayers with the sign of the cross is a profound gesture that expresses who we are, whose we are, and what we believe. To begin our prayer with the sign of the cross is not a prelude to prayer but is a prayer in and of itself.

(4) A Greeting and Invitation to Prayer—In order for the assembly to pray well together, it helps if they feel at home with one another and with the prayer they are about to enter into. As the prayer begins, it is more than a nicety to greet and welcome into the prayer those who are praying. The greeting is a reminder that God is extending the invitation, and, through our prayer, we are about to respond.

(5) Scripture—In liturgical prayer, the word of God is nonnegotiable. If we want to hear God's voice, we must listen to the word of God proclaimed in our midst. It is acceptable to include readings from inspirational literature or from the writings and speeches of great figures, but these should never overshadow the living word of God that comes to us in Scripture.

(6) Ritual Gesture—Liturgical prayer is sacramental, which means that it involves ritual movement and gesture. Processing around the room (children especially love "parades!") with the Bible, coming forward to bless ourselves with holy water, sharing a sign of Christ's peace, blessing one another on the forehead, and so on are all opportunities to pray with our entire bodies.

> " Liturgical prayer is sacramental . . . "

(7) Responses and Shared Prayer—As mentioned earlier, be sure to pay attention to the role of the assembly. Provide opportunities for your participants to respond to the Scripture readings with a responsorial psalm or other form of prayer. Include traditional prayers that the assembly can pray together in unison, such as the Lord's Prayer, the Hail Mary, the Memorare, the Confiteor, and other prayers that are appropriate for the occasion. It is also important to include spontaneous prayer, such as the sharing of petitions, so that your participants know that—even in formal prayer—speaking with God can be informal.

(8) The Liturgical Calendar—Be sure to look to the church's liturgical calendar for guidance. The season or feast that the church is celebrating will provide clues as to how to prepare the environment, which readings to choose, and what prayers to include. Using prayers from the Sacramentary (such as, the opening prayer of that day's liturgy) or from the Liturgy of the Hours serves to bind your group's liturgical prayer more closely to the liturgical prayer of the universal church.

(9) Length and Pace of the Prayer—A prayer service that is either rushed or dragging along can affect how "at home" participants feel about the prayer experience. Consider your age group as well. Small children have very short attention spans and cannot sit still for very long. Older children may have longer attention spans but still need variety.

By leading others in liturgical prayer, we help to prepare them for the celebration of the Eucharist—the source and summit of the Christian life. For more information about the Mass, see my book *Living the Mass: How One Hour a Week Can Change Your Life* (Loyola Press, 2005). We cannot love God with our head alone. Through prayer, we learn to love God with our whole heart, soul, mind, and strength.

7. **Teaching Spontaneous Prayer**—With our rich treasury of traditional prayers, Catholics are sometimes unfamiliar with spontaneous prayer. You can help your participants become more comfortable with spontaneous prayer by encouraging them to follow these steps.

a. **Address God**—God answers to many names, so any title of honor will do. (For example: Dear God, Heavenly Father, Almighty God, Dear Jesus, Creator of All Things, or Loving God.)

b. **Offer Thanks**—It's always good to begin prayer by being thankful. It reminds us that God provides for us. Help your participants to offer thanks for simple things. (For example: Thank you for bringing us together today. Thank you for the summer vacation

> " It's always good to begin prayer by being thankful. "

Offering a spontaneous prayer can be simple. Follow these steps.

1. **Address God**   4. **Pray for the needs of the group**

2. **Give thanks**   5. **Pray for the needs of others**

3. **Ask for forgiveness** 6. **Conclude: Amen**

that we just enjoyed. Thank you for helping us to learn about our confirmation.)

c. **Ask for Forgiveness**—In private, you might ask for forgiveness for a wrong you have committed. When praying for a group, a leader can ask forgiveness for our general sinfulness. (For example: We're sorry for the times that we don't follow your word. Please forgive us for the times that we think only of ourselves.)

d. **Pray for the Needs of the Group**—Typically, a group is gathered for a purpose. The simplest thing to pray for is success for the purpose of that gathering. (For example: Open our minds and hearts so that we will learn about you today. Inspire us so that we make wise choices about our service projects.)

e. **Pray for the Needs of Others**—We never simply pray for ourselves, but wc think of the needs of others. (For example: We pray for all those who are sick and unable to be with us today. We pray for the homeless on this very cold day. We pray for an end to the violence in our world.)

f. **Conclude**—A simple phrase indicates that the prayer is ending. (For example: We ask this through Christ our Lord. We ask this in Jesus' name. Amen.)

> "For prayer is nothing else than being on terms of friendship with God."
>
> —St. Teresa of Ávila

Ritual—A ritual is a habitual way of doing something. In prayer, rituals include symbolic ways of acknowledging God's power. Blessing ourselves with holy water is a habitual way (ritual) of acknowledging God's saving grace in baptism. A ritual is effective because it goes beyond words and relies on symbols and metaphors. The more we use them, the more familiar and meaningful they become.

Meditation—Meditation, or reflective prayer, is thinking about God, often with the aid of a Scripture passage, an inspirational reading, or sacred images. When we meditate, we attempt to become aware of—and "plug into"—God's power and presence in our lives.

Contemplation—Contemplation is simply resting quietly in God's presence. In contemplation, one does not attempt to speak to God but simply marvels at his glorious presence. It can be compared to enjoying a beautiful piece of art or a nature scene. No words are needed.

Prayer—Prayer is time spent in awareness of God's presence. Prayer is *always* a response to God. God has already acted in our lives. Through prayer, we are acknowledging and responding to God's saving presence. Even when we offer petitions, we are doing so in response to the fact that God has previously touched our lives. We are acknowledging this fact and asking God to do so once again. The *Catechism of the Catholic Church* teaches us that "prayer is the raising of one's mind and heart to God" (2559).

Troubleshooting

⊕ **Like electricity, the power of prayer is nothing to take lightly.** Prayer is powerful. Be prepared for the fact that the power of God may touch one of your participants in an unexpected way (e.g., a participant begins crying during a prayer experience). Recognize it as part of the prayer experience.

- **Leading others, especially children, in prayer is not easy.** By the same token, it is not rocket science. In many cases, you may very well be introducing your participants to the concept of prayer. Start small. Start simple. Prayers of thanksgiving are often a good place to start because everyone can think of at least *one* thing that they are thankful for.

> **The power of prayer is nothing to take lightly.**

- **Be patient.** Some people can be uncomfortable with prayer. Children can also be immature about it. Don't give up. Employ simple rituals (such as an enthronement of the Bible in silence before each session) that do not require a great deal of time and concentration. Use them regularly so that your participants develop a sense of prayerfulness.

- **Avoid the temptation of saying that you have no time to pray because you have so much content to teach.** Prayer is a part of the content of our faith as well. Remember, it is one of the four "pillars" of the *Catechism of the Catholic Church*, along with the creed, the sacraments, and the commandments. We are never too busy to grab a bite to eat, even if it's fast food. To skip prayer is to skip the all-important reminder that all that we do is in acknowledgment of God.

High Praise from a Fifth-Grade Boy—A True Story

A substitute catechist walked into a fifth-grade class. A boy confronted her and asked, "Who are you?" She introduced herself and explained that she was the substitute. The boy said, "That's fine, but you should know that I don't believe in God." The catechist smiled and asked him to take a seat with the group, which he did. In the course of the class, she introduced the concept of reflective prayer and led the fifth graders in a meditation. When the class was over, the boy came up to her and asked, "Are you going to be here next week?" When she responded yes, he said, "Good." Then he asked, "Are we going to do more of this prayer stuff?" Again, when she responded yes, he said, "Good." Then he left. From a fifth-grade boy, that was a major display of emotion and a high form of praise! The catechist realized that the way into this young man's faith life was through his heart and that prayer was the vehicle to reach that destination.

Scripture

*"Rising very early before dawn, he
left and went off to a deserted place,
where he prayed."*

(Mark 1:35)

Prayer

Lord Jesus, you made prayer a regular part of your life and ministry. Time and again, the Scriptures tell us that you went off alone to pray. You knew that the Creator was your source of power. You knew that prayer was your link to the power of the Creator. Help me to realize the power of prayer in my life and in the life of my participants. Teach us all to pray so that we may acknowledge your power and glory and be energized by your grace.

For an opportunity to companion with other catechists and to nourish our vocation, visit www.catechistsjourney.com.

Chapter Ten

Sandpaper: Smoothing Out Discipline Problems

When doing home improvements, we want our finished products to look smooth and neat. However, many of the materials we are working with are rough and rugged. After filling cracks in a wall, we still find that the surface is rough and needs to be smoothed out. After cutting a piece of wood, we find that the edges are rough and need to be smoothed out. This is where sandpaper comes in. If it were not for sandpaper, we would run the risk of bumpy surfaces and splinters. When we use a sander to smooth down a surface, it seems like a miracle is taking place.

> "Young people today . . . will be very likely to reject some of what they learn, or to refuse to integrate it in their lives, if it is not taught in ways that make sense to them emotionally, spiritually, and intellectually."
>
> *NATIONAL DIRECTORY FOR CATECHESIS*, 4C

Rough Edges in Catechesis: Discipline Problems

We tend to have a somewhat romantic notion of being a catechist. We picture ourselves speaking eloquently as participants interact joyfully and enthusiastically with us and with one another. And then, of course, there is reality. In catechesis, we encounter any number of rough edges. One of the rough edges we face is that of discipline problems—especially in catechesis with children and adolescents. Left unchecked, discipline problems can be like pieces of wood that are not sanded—they can cause some pain. A good catechist learns how to smooth out discipline problems. Maintaining discipline in the catechetical setting allows the beauty of the participants and the power of God's word to show through: just

as sanding down a surface brings out the true beauty of a piece of wood. Rather than giving up when faced with discipline problems, learn how to use some tools to smooth them out.

Discipline is a necessary part of faith formation. Each Lent, we practice the disciplines of prayer, fasting, and giving alms. The idea is that, in order to be a disciple of Jesus, one needs discipline. Remember, our God is "not the God of disorder but of peace" (1 Corinthians 14:33). When you maintain discipline in your learning environment, you are acting in the image of God—in whose name you teach.

★ ★

Jesus himself faced some rather difficult situations.

- ★ *Matthew 13:57* (Jesus is rejected in his hometown.)
- ★ *Mark 11:28* (The crowds challenge Jesus' authority.)
- ★ *Luke 4:29* (Jesus is thrown out of the synagogue and dragged to a cliff.)
- ★ *Luke 9:52–53* (A Samaritan town refuses to receive Jesus.)
- ★ *Luke 19:7* (The crowds grumble when Jesus announces he will dine with Zacchaeus.)
- ★ *John 6:66* (Many of Jesus' followers find his teaching too difficult and leave him.)
- ★ *John 8:59* (Crowds pick up stones to throw at Jesus.)
- ★ *John 9:14* (The crowds challenge Jesus' healing of a man born blind.)
- ★ *John 10:31* (More stones!)

★ ★

By the way, have you noticed the similarities between the words *discipline* and *disciple*? They both share the same root word, which means "to learn." In other words, as a catechist, you are responsible for keeping discipline so that disciples can learn how to follow Jesus.

Skills, Tips, and Practical Advice for Maintaining Discipline

1. **Understand the Role of Discipline**—Good discipline is not an end in itself. The goal of your session is effective learning. One can have good discipline but still have a poor lesson. The role of good discipline is to remove any obstacles from an effective learning experience.

> **The role of good discipline is to remove any obstacles from an effective learning experience.**

2. **Identify the Improper Behavior**—One doesn't need to sand down an entire wall before painting. Only the rough spots need to be sanded down. By the same token, be sure to clearly identify the discipline problems that you need to address. As the old saying goes, "choose your battles wisely." Once you have clearly identified the discipline problems that are most troublesome, you can develop a plan for addressing them. When identifying discipline problems, consider the following causes of improper behavior:

   ◆ boredom
   ◆ immaturity and ego needs (seeking attention, trying to impress peers)
   ◆ hostility toward either you, other participants, the church, or parents (some hostility can be considered natural for certain age groups)
   ◆ personality clash (with you or other participants)
   ◆ emotional problem (family situation, drug related, guilt, inner conflict)
   ◆ the "nature" of religious formation (young people, especially pre-adolescents and early adolescents, don't want their peers to think that they enjoy religion)

3. **Don't Panic**—When discipline problems arise, strive to remain calm and in control. Communicating a sense of authority while remaining calm is not only effective but also necessary in developing a long-term strategy for combating discipline problems. Losing your cool may work for the moment, but it undermines your credibility in the long run.

4. **Avoid Interrupting Your Lesson**—One of the reasons children and adolescents misbehave is because they know that their disruption will interrupt the flow of the lesson, frustrate you, and bring attention to them. A good catechist learns to deal with discipline problems without stopping the lesson. By using eye contact, placing a hand on the participant's desk or tabletop, or standing next to the "culprit" while you continue to facilitate the lesson, you can minimize the behavior without interrupting the flow of your lesson.

5. **Keep Participants Involved**—When participants get bored, they try to create their own stimulation. When you see that a participant's attention is wavering, involve him or her in the lesson by asking a question or by giving the participant a task to perform. By keeping your participants busy and on task right from the start, you eliminate a great deal of potential trouble.

> "Be ever engaged, so that whenever the devil calls he may find you occupied."
> —St. Jerome

6. **Ride Your Eye, Use Names, and Move Around**—If you are completely stationary as a catechist, you invite participants farthest away from you to engage in misbehavior. Stay on the move. Walk around the room as you teach and keep your eyes moving around as you speak. If you are answering one participant's question, move your eyes around the room so that it is clear you are still speaking to everyone. Most importantly, learn and use your participants' names. One of the most effective ways of getting a participant's attention is to call his or her name out loud, pause, and direct the question or task to that person.

> A good catechist learns to deal with discipline problems without stopping the lesson.

7. **Check Your Seating Arrangement**—How a room is arranged can have a great impact on behavior. Your seating should be arranged in such a way that no participant feels separated or remote from the hub of activity. If a participant feels he or she can "hide" from you, he or she will take advantage of the situation. Make sure visual lines are open. Likewise, if a participant is misbehaving, it could be that he or she is sitting with others who are egging the participant on. Moving a participant's seat can effectively reduce bad behavior.

> " How a room is arranged can have a great impact on behavior. "

8. **Reinforce Good Behavior**—Don't just focus on the negative. Learn to focus attention on good behavior, and reinforce it. When participants are behaving properly, you can reward them with affirmations. When a participant who is prone to misbehaving shows the proper behavior, be sure to reinforce it with a positive affirmation—without going overboard.

9. **Make a Few Rules, Explain, and Enforce Them Consistently**—When you first begin meeting with your group, it is a good idea to formulate some rules with the help of the participants. Depending upon the age of your participants, you should be able to ask them what rules they will need to make the gatherings go well and to create a good learning environment. Later, when enforcing the rules, you can remind them that these are their rules. Be sure participants know clearly what the rules are. Also, you should enforce them in a consistent manner so the participants know that the rules are to be taken seriously.

> " You will accomplish more by kind words and a courteous manner than by anger or sharp rebuke, which should never be used except in necessity. "
> —St. Angela Merici

10. **Get to Know the Age Group You Work With**—Be sure to get to know about the developmental characteristics of the age group you are working with. Some behaviors can be more easily understood and dealt with if you have a working knowledge of the physical, psychological, emotional, social, moral, and spiritual characteristics of the age group. Most catechist manuals include an overview of these developmental characteristics.

11. **Avoid the Following:**

    ◆ When working with children, never send a child out of the room alone and unsupervised, lest he or she wander off or even leave the building.

    ◆ Be careful not to use God as an "enforcer." Some catechists use the "good cop/bad cop" routine and make God the "bad cop." This creates a theology of God that is not consistent with our heritage. Children do not need an image of an angry God waiting to dish out punishment for bad behavior.

    ◆ Avoid being overly tough: you run the risk of alienating your participants. They may be so intimidated by you that they will either not respond at all or will simply parrot back to you what they think you want to hear. Recall that religious education is, for many participants, their most significant experience of the church. If it is a negative experience, or one that they fear, they may carry that with them for years to come.

"I need you to line up by attention span."

12. **Working with Small Groups**—Discipline problems often arise when participants are arranged in small groups to complete a task. Here are some tips for working more effectively with small groups:

- Explain the purpose for arranging your participants into groups. Provide clear instructions and directions before arranging them into groups and before distributing any necessary supplies. Ask for volunteers to repeat the instructions and directions out loud so that you know they understand their task.

- Employ creative and fun techniques for grouping your participants so as to engage them in the process. Use groups as a way for participants to get to know one another and to move out of their usual circles. Groups of four are ideal for effectiveness. Arrange the room so that groups can work together without disrupting other groups.

- Give brief and concise time limits for completing the task. Create a sense of urgency by allowing slightly less time than might be needed to complete the task. You can always allow an extra minute or two if the groups are not ready when the original time is up.

> **Create a sense of urgency by allowing slightly less time than might be needed to complete assigned tasks.**

- Provide a signal that will indicate when the groups are to quiet themselves and return their attention to the large group. Keep the participants on task by walking around and asking groups to tell you how far along they are.

- Be sure that the group work cannot be completed by any one participant but truly requires each one to assume responsibility for a task. Assign roles such as leader, recorder, reporter, monitor (keeps track of time), and collector (collects materials and supplies). Include a high level of individual accountability. For example, if a group of four is to brainstorm a list of ten things, make sure every member contributes at least two suggestions. If one participant appears to be dominating a group, gently intervene to invite other members of the group to contribute.

- Provide ongoing feedback (affirmations and challenges, as needed) as they continue their work. Likewise, provide time estimates so that the participants know how to pace themselves. Tell them where they should be in completing their task and encourage them to arrive at definite conclusions.

◆ Make sure that the results of the group work are observable and concrete. For example, if praticipants are to brainstorm lists, make sure that each group has someone recording the list on a piece of paper. Allow groups to report on their work and make use of their findings. Bring closure to group activities by asking volunteers to summarize what was accomplished by group work.

Glossary

Discipline problems may be cataloged into three distinct categories.

Minor Discipline Problems—These are the most typical problems that a catechist faces, such as wavering attention, distractions, and side talking. While none of these may seem overly serious, they can wear down a catechist. Furthermore, left unchecked, they can erode the discipline of a group and lead to more serious problems.

Moderate Discipline Problems—These are problems that can seriously disrupt the flow of your lesson, such as participants who set themselves off from the group and refuse to participate, simple mischief such as throwing small objects or paper airplanes, and talking out of turn. Although it is more difficult to deal with these problems without interrupting the flow of your lesson, you can still deal with these situations effectively without bringing your lesson to a grinding halt.

Major Discipline Problems—These are problems that can bring your lesson crashing down around you. For example, you might have a learning activity that dissolves into total chaos due to lack of clear directions; a participant "sabotaging" a lesson by interfering with a piece of equipment such as a VCR/DVD player; or an incident of dishonesty or disrespect such as stealing or racially motivated graffiti. In all instances, it is important to remain calm and in control. You need to be able to deal with the specific behavior in a manner that will maintain self-respect for you and for your group.

Catechist: Kim, I hope I didn't see you copying from Nikki's paper!

Kim: I hope you didn't see me either!

Troubleshooting

- **In a serious situation, it is crucial that you consult your catechetical leader, principal, pastor, colleague, or any other person of authority.** This way, you will not have to face the situation alone.

- **On the other hand, you cannot run to these people every time some discipline problem arises.** Be sure the situation warrants it.

- **In a serious situation, be fair and flexible, and always give the participant an opportunity to redeem him- or herself.** Negotiating a contract is a way of dealing with the behavior in a concrete and authoritative manner while providing the participant with an opportunity to work his or her way out of the bad behavior.

- **Make sure that no activity begins until everyone is "on the same page."** This means being sure that all rules and directions (as well as consequences for violating them) are understood and clarified before you begin any activity.

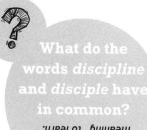

What do the words *discipline* and *disciple* have in common?

They both came from the Latin discere, meaning "to learn."

Scripture

"Endure your trials as 'discipline'; God treats you as sons. For what 'son' is there whom his father does not discipline? . . . At the time, all discipline seems a cause not for joy but for pain, yet later it brings the peaceful fruit of righteousness to those who are trained by it."

(HEBREWS 12:7, 11)

Prayer

Sometimes I get worried about facing challenging situations in my teaching. Lord Jesus, you faced some pretty tough audiences in your day. Yet you stayed focused on preaching the Good News of the kingdom of God. Grant me the patience, fairness, and perspective that I need to maintain my focus, and to face up to these challenges and handle them with calmness and authority. In all things, allow me to show love, no matter how frustrated I may become. Help me to acquire new skills to handle challenges so that your word may come to life in my participants.

For an opportunity to companion with other catechists and to nourish our vocation, visit www.catechistsjourney.com.

Chapter Eleven

Furniture Polish: Polishing Your Technique

> "Because catechists are witnesses to Jesus Christ in the Church and in the world, their ongoing formation is to . . . equip them to proclaim the truth of Jesus Christ boldly and enthusiastically."
>
> *National Directory for Catechesis*, 55E

Most home-improvement jobs create dust. Typically, when I am done with a home-improvement project, the room I am working in (as well as surrounding areas) is often covered in a layer of dust. It's at this point that a good furniture polish comes in very handy. With a trusty dust rag in hand, I can gather up the dust left behind by my work and (with a little furniture polish) bring out the shine of the tables, chairs, cabinets, and countertops in the room. It's amazing what a little furniture polish can do to make things look fresh and new.

Polishing Your Teaching Techniques

Many of us begin our work as catechists feeling stiff and inadequate. If only we had the polished approach that the veteran catechist has as he or she glides through sessions with poise and savvy.

A visitor to a joke factory was going on a tour around the plant. As he was being led along, he heard the foreman call out over the loudspeaker, "Number seventy-two." This was followed by a great big roar of laughter from the workers. After another minute, he heard another announcement: "Number sixteen." Again, loud guffaws of laughter came from the workers. The visitor asked the tour guide, "What are they laughing at?" The tour guide explained, "The jokes are coded by number. When the foreman calls out a number, everyone recognizes the joke and that's why they laugh." The visitor asked, "Can I try it?" "Sure," replied the tour guide. So the visitor went up to the microphone and called out "Number sixty-eight." Nothing. No reaction. No laughter. "What happened?" he asked. The tour guide replied, "Well, I guess some people have a better technique than others."

It's true that some people seem to have a very polished technique when it comes to telling jokes while others do not. When it comes to being a catechist, we sometimes feel the same way. Unfortunately, we often feel like the visitor to the joke factory, wondering what we lack when it comes to technique. The fact is, just as most people can learn to tell a joke properly, most new catechists can polish the skills and techniques needed to become more effective as a catechist.

Step-by-Step Instructions for Polishing Your Technique

1. **Move Around**—Moving around the room helps to keep participants on their toes and expresses a sense of energy and enthusiasm. I once knew a teacher who would stand up on top of his desk every so often to emphasize a point. You may not need to be this drastic, but you should certainly consider moving about in a way that you feel comfortable and that communicates energy and enthusiasm.

> ❝ We are what we repeatedly do. Exellence, therefore, is not an act, but a habit. ❞
> —Aristotle

2. **Make Eye Contact/Ride Your Eye**—Your eyes should follow the same rule as your body—move around. As you move about the room, make sure your eyes are riding around the group so that all participants know that you are aware of them and interested in engaging them in the lesson. This is also a great way of preventing misbehavior. By (almost) having eyes in the back of your head, you keep participants on task.

3. **Vary Your Voice**—Nothing is more boring to learners than a monotonous voice. Put some energy into your voice. Use it as a tool to make a point or to add authority and enthusiasm to your lesson. Vary the sound of your voice to make sure that it is not monotonous. If your own voice does not communicate interest in your topic, then you have little chance of getting the participants interested.

> If we are truly preaching and teaching the Good News, then our faces and body language must reflect it.

4. **Be Aware of Facial Expression and Body Language**—People, especially children, are very in tune with facial expressions and body language. If we are truly preaching and teaching the Good News, then our faces and body language must reflect it. If our facial expressions and body language (including the way we dress) express the fact that we are tired, bored, irritated, or uninterested, then we are shooting ourselves in the foot.

> **"It is not fitting, when one is in God's service, to have a gloomy face or a chilling look."**
> —St. Francis of Assisi

Use facial expression and body language as a way of communicating to your participants that you truly have "good news" for them. One of the best ways to determine your movement, pace, voice, and facial expression is to have a colleague videotape you while you are teaching a lesson. Afterward, sit down with this colleague and assess your style.

5. **Vary Your Pace**—Any runner will tell you that it is important to have a healthy pace for a distance run. Go too fast, and you'll run out of steam. Go too slow, and you lose. The same is true of your lesson. An effective lesson relies on a varied pace. Be sure to keep an eye on the time to make sure you're not spending too much time on one segment at the expense of others. By the same token, if you are moving too quickly, slow down and include more detailed information to fill in the time.

6. **Keep a Sense of Humor**—You don't have to become a comedian or an entertainer to be a good catechist; however, most people want to have fun. Humor is a way of celebrating, and, as Christians, we celebrate the Good News of Jesus. A few light moments in your lessons can make participants feel at home and comfortable.

> One of the best ways to determine your movement, pace, voice, facial expression, etc., is to have a colleague videotape you while you are teaching a lesson. Afterward, sit down with this colleague and assess your style.

Appreciate the humor that your participants can offer and don't feel shy about adding your own. Strive to be professionally delightful. One can keep order and focus as a catechist and still maintain a sense of humor.

7. **Be Aware**—Hockey legend Wayne Gretzky was not the biggest or the fastest skater of all time. Yet, he holds almost every scoring record in the book. When asked how he accomplished such great feats, he explained that he had a knack for knowing where the puck was going and made sure he was there before anyone else. In other words, he

had an awareness of what was going on and was able to anticipate the next move. Some people claimed he was lucky. The truth is, his awareness put him in the right place at the right time. An awareness of how your lesson is unfolding and how your participants are reacting is an important skill that will assist you in communicating the right thing at the right time.

> "Chance favors the prepared mind."
> —Louis Pasteur

8. **Walk the Line between Creativity and Maintenance—**
Too much innovation can be disconcerting to participants who need to have a sense of order and regularity. By the same token, however, many participants need to have their creative juices constantly stirred. The effective catechist learns to move between the two poles of innovation and sameness, and achieve a balance and a healthy tension.

"Stop me if you've heard this one before."

9. **Strive to Be Not Only Effective, but Also Affective**—Jesus taught us to love the Lord God "with all your heart, with all your soul, with all your mind, and with all your strength" (Mark 12:30). This means that our love for God must penetrate beyond the intellectual level and involve all of our being, including our emotions (our affect). This is not to say that, as a catechist, you have to wear your heart on your sleeve. Rather, it means not being afraid to express the emotions that are involved in discipleship.

Catholic Tradition describes the fruits of the Holy Spirit as visible expressions of the presence of the Spirit. "The tradition of the Church lists twelve of them: 'charity, joy, peace, patience, kindness, goodness, generosity, gentleness, faithfulness, modesty, self-control, chastity'" (*Catechism of the Catholic Church*, 1832). These are not superficial emotions but are deep-seated dispositions. The affective catechist knows that the light of Christ must not be hidden under a bushel but must be displayed for all to see.

Glossary

Feedback—When a microphone is too close to a speaker, it amplifies itself. The result is feedback. As a catechist, you can use feedback to "amplify yourself." Feedback is a way to get a better look at yourself and your teaching skills. You can obtain feedback either through analysis of video-or audiotape, or by observation from a peer. With the proper feedback, you can effectively polish your techniques.

Presence—Some people have good stage presence, which means that their posture, movement, voice, and facial expression all appear very natural. As a catechist, you need to work on your presence so that it is an authentic and effective expression of your desire to proclaim God's word.

Troubleshooting

⊕ **As you attempt to polish your technique, don't try to become something or someone that you're not.** Polished presence must go hand in hand with sincerity. Young people especially are very perceptive when it comes to behavior that is fake. Stay within your comfort zone but gently push the boundaries out so that you become adventuresome.

> **"** If the truth were self-evident, eloquence would be unnecessary. **"**
> —Cicero

⊕ **Think back to the joke factory story at the beginning of this chapter— some have it and some don't.** God has given you gifts and limitations. Become aware of them. Accentuate the positive. Play to your strengths. Highlight and improve upon the best that you have. Accept your limitations. As hard as we may try, some of us will just never be the next Bishop Sheen.

For an opportunity to companion with other catechists and to nourish our vocation, visit www.catechistsjourney.com.

Chapter Twelve

Instruction Manuals: Using Textbooks and Catechist Manuals

When I have to fix an electrical problem around the house, I get pretty nervous—so does my wife. She's convinced that I will either fry myself or blow up the house. I fear I may accomplish both. You can imagine, then, that when I have to complete some electrical work around the house, my handy home-improvement manual is nearby and my wife is far away. With my manual on hand, I'm able to read and follow the instructions. I can then work effectively to get the job done.

> "Catechist and teacher manuals are essential components of any sound catechetical textbook series."
>
> *National Directory for Catechesis,* 68a

Using Catechetical Texts and Manuals

A textbook is a tool. It is one of many tools available to you. The effective catechist recognizes that a textbook is a means to an end, not an end in and of itself. When doing my electrical repairs, I could memorize the directions in my home-improvement manual; but unless I took my nose out of the book and went to work applying the theory and suggested procedures, my electrical repairs would never get done. The same is true in our lessons. The goal of a lesson is not to cover a text but to invite our participants into an experience of Jesus.

> Take the time to go through the entire textbook to become familiar with the overall theme as well as the unit and chapter themes.

Skills, Tips, and Practical Advice for Using Textbooks and Catechist Manuals

Luckily for us, many excellent catechetical texts and manuals are available to serve as resources in our ministry. Let's take a look at some tips for using texts and catechist manuals more effectively.

1. **Familiarize Yourself with Your Text**—Take the time to go through the entire textbook to become familiar with the overall theme, as well as the unit and chapter themes. Most catechist manuals include a scope and sequence that identifies what doctrine is being presented in each grade throughout the series. It helps to know what was taught previously and what is going to be taught next year and beyond.

2. **Be Aware of Your Participants' Level of Aptitude**—Be sure your text is appropriate for the age level and aptitude of your participants. Your catechetical leader or principal will no doubt play an important role in this, but you are the one in the trenches. As a catechist, be sure that your text is a tool that will assist, not frustrate, your participants. Furthermore, most catechist manuals include materials that help you to understand the developmental aspects (physical, social, psychological, moral, and spiritual) of the age group you are working with. Read up on this background information so that you are more in tune with your learners.

> "A book is a garden, an orchard, a storehouse, a party, a company by the way, a counselor, a multitude of counselors."
> —HENRY WARD BEECHER

3. **Preview the Material You Plan to Cover**—Some catechetical texts are so good that they can lull us into a false sense of complacency. Beware of this. Preview the material you plan to cover to ensure that it is an effective lesson. Strive to memorize the learning outcomes for the session you are about to teach so that they are at the tip of your tongue. Look through current newspapers and magazines for stories and pictures that relate to the theme of your lesson.

4. **Give Your Participants an Overview of What They Are about to Read**—Catechists commonly make the mistake of beginning a lesson with the instructions. For example, "Open your book to page 35. Can I have a volunteer to read?" First of all, the participants have no notion of what the goal for the lesson is other than to read the text. Second, the participants have no concept of what they are supposed to pay attention to or look for in the text. When reading or working on a section of a text, an introduction and a brief overview of what you are about to read or do is required. This helps the participants become predisposed to paying attention.

> "The instruction we find in books is like fire. We fetch it from our neighbors, kindle it at home, communicate it to others, and it becomes the property of all."
> —VOLTAIRE

5. **Vary Your Approaches to Reading the Text**—The material in a text can be accessed in a variety of ways.

   ◆ Volunteers can read it aloud.
   ◆ The participants can read a section quietly and then report on what they have read.
   ◆ Participants can be placed in pairs and, after quietly reading a section, can interview one another to get a summary of the sections.

   > " Reading is to the mind what exercise is to the body. "
   > —JOSEPH ADDISON

   ◆ A "jigsaw" is a format that breaks a long text into smaller parts. Sections of the text are assigned to various small groups to read. Then they report back to the large group what they have read. When each group has completed its reporting, it is as if a giant jigsaw puzzle has been put together by your entire group.

6. **Identify Vocabulary Words and Key Phrases**—If your catechist manual has not already done so, identify words that should become part of your participants' vocabulary, as well as key phrases or ideas that should be highlighted. Previewing your text ahead of time allows you to identify these words and phrases and place them on the board for quick reference.

7. **Be Aware of the Pace**—Reading a text can slow down the pace of your lesson. Break up the reading of text sections so that they are interspersed with activities and discussions that will keep your participants alert.

> Use the text and catechist manual as a springboard for adding your own discussion questions and learning activities.

8. **Carefully Look Over the Catechist Notes in the Margin**—Most catechist manuals provide liner notes or a section in the margin of each page containing background on the text and suggestions for discussing and exploring the content. These catechist notes can provide you with some excellent ideas for making the text come alive and connecting it with your participants' lives.

9. **Develop Additional Questions and Activities**—Use the text and catechist manual as a springboard for adding your own discussion questions and learning activities. Use the graphics (photographs, pictures, and artwork) in your text to generate additional questions and discussion. Look over any blackline masters that are provided as supplements to your lesson and determine when and how they can be most effectively used.

> "It is the supreme art of the teacher to awaken joy in creative expression and knowledge."
> —Albert Einstein

Glossary

Content—Like a bottle holding its contents of water, sugar, food coloring, or preserves, every lesson has its contents as well. The content of your lesson is all the teachings of the church, given to us by Jesus. This content is to be integrated into the lives of your participants. The text, however, is only one tool and should not be seen as the sole source of content.

Catechist Manuals—If you do not have one, get one. Most catechetical texts are accompanied by a catechist manual that provides you with a step-by-step outline for the entire lesson. It also includes ideas that invite the participants to engage in off-the-page activities.

Annotated Text—Some programs do not have a full catechist manual. Instead, they provide an annotated text or a copy of the participants' text with keywords and ideas highlighted or underlined. They also include suggested questions for discussion in the margins.

Troubleshooting

+ **Without proper planning, you may find yourself well into a lesson before you realize that a text may be outdated, dull, ineffective, or biased.** If this occurs, be prepared to move away from the text and into an activity or discussion that will be more in line with the learning outcomes you have planned for the lesson. Always have Plan B ready.

> *" Catechetical aids . . . aim to give those who use them a better knowledge of the mysteries of Christ, aimed at true conversion and a life more in conformity with God's will. "*
>
> *GENERAL DIRECTORY FOR CATECHESIS*, 283

+ **Some participants cannot read well.** Never allow a participant to be embarrassed by forcing him or her to read a text he or she is incapable of reading. If a participant is stumbling through a section out loud, gently help him or her through it. Then ask for someone to assist by taking over the reading. Take note of a participant's reading difficulties and encourage the parents to work with him or her, or ask another participant to assist through tutoring.

Scripture

"He came to Nazareth, where he had grown up, and went according to his custom into the synagogue on the sabbath day. He stood up to read and was handed a scroll of the prophet Isaiah. He unrolled the scroll and found the passage where it was written:
*   'The Spirit of the Lord is upon me . . .'"*

(LUKE 4:16–18)

Prayer

Lord, when you entered the synagogue in Galilee, you were handed the text, and you read from the prophet Isaiah. But you didn't stop there. You added a new insight or twist to the centuries-old text and stirred up a great deal of controversy. Help me to go beyond the texts that are handed to me and stir up something of interest to my participants, so that they, too, may be challenged. Help me to use the texts assigned to me as a catalyst or stepping stone to the fullness of your word—a word that does not simply fill space on a page but has the capacity to change lives forever.

For an opportunity to companion with other catechists and to nourish our vocation, visit www.catechistsjourney.com.

Chapter Thirteen

Samples and Illustrations:
Looking to the Bible for Vision

When I'm working on a home-improvement project, I often refer to self-help manuals or samples from a store so that I can get an idea of what the finished product is supposed to look like. The pictures illustrate the fact that someone has attempted this particular project before, and I can learn from his or her experience. Samples provide me with an idea of what is available. After I've had an opportunity to visualize the end product, I am better able to get to work. I now have a vision of what I am striving to complete. My finished product may not look exactly like the picture in the book, but, if it's close, I feel like I've been successful.

> "Catechesis should take Sacred Scripture as its inspiration, its fundamental curriculum, and its end because it strengthens faith, nourishes the soul, and nurtures the spiritual life."
>
> *NATIONAL DIRECTORY FOR CATECHESIS,* 24B

The Bible Provides a Vision

In catechesis, we are helping others to envision life as a disciple of Jesus. What does that look like? It would help if we had some illustrations, photographs, diagrams, or samples that could show our participants an image of what the life of a disciple of Christ is supposed to look like. This is where the Bible comes in. The Bible provides us with numerous images of what it looks like when human beings respond to God's call and live a life of faith. Our lives are not the same as the lives of the people that we encounter in the Bible. Yet, their stories can act as illustrative guides for us so that we can make the adaptations we need to respond to God in our lives.

Skills, Tips, and Practical Advice for Using the Bible in Catechesis

1. **Familiarize Yourself with the Bible**—If you wish to introduce participants to the Bible, make sure that you yourself are becoming familiar with the Bible. While it's nice to have a large decorative Bible enthroned in your home, it is also helpful to have a smaller, softcover New American Bible (the translation used in the Lectionary) that you can use (and highlight and take notes in) as your personal copy. Ask your catechetical leader, principal, or pastor to assist you in acquiring one. A good introduction to the Bible is my book *God's Library: A Catholic Introduction to the World's Greatest Book* (Loyola Press, 2005).

   > A father was reading Bible stories to his young son. He read, "The man named Lot was warned to take his wife and flee out of the city, but his wife looked back and was turned to salt." His son asked, "What happened to the flea?"

2. **Read and Pray the Bible**—The best way to get to know the Bible is to begin reading it and praying with it on your own. However, don't read the Bible as you would other books (i.e., beginning on page one and trying to get all the way through to the last page). Since the Bible is a collection of books, you can begin with any book that you are attracted to. Exodus, Psalms, the Gospel of Mark, and the Acts of the Apostles are good places to begin. You can read a brief passage each day or several days per week.

   A good introduction to the Bible is my book *God's Library: A Catholic Introduction to the World's Greatest Book* (Loyola Press, 2005).

Steps for Reading and Praying the Bible

a. Set a prayerful, quiet mood.

b. Pray to the Holy Spirit to open up your mind and heart to the word of God.

c. Read the passage once slowly. Look over any footnotes and commentary that will assist your understanding of the passage.

d. Go back and read the passage again, this time more slowly and prayerfully. If the passage describes a story or event, use your imagination to place yourself within the scene as a participant. Pause at phrases, words, or images that speak to you and allow them to resonate. Whereas your first read-through is for the head, this one is for the heart.

e. Be quiet. Let the word of God continue to echo in your heart, mind, and soul.

f. Pray in your own words. Thank God for the word and ask for the grace you need to apply it to your life.

3. **Enthrone the Bible in Your Learning Space**—Make sure that the Bible is in a prominent place (e.g., in the center, directly in front, or in a special corner) in your room. To "enthrone" the Bible means to place it so that it has a look of prominence and honor in the room. Putting it on a stand with a candle and cross nearby creates a sacred space that your participants will develop reverence for. Use tablecloths and fabrics that reflect the colors of the liturgical seasons so that participants see the Bible as connected to the celebration of the Eucharist.

> You don't have to be a Bible expert to be an effective catechist. You simply need to be dedicated to learning more about God as revealed in the Bible.

4. **Arrange for Bibles in Your Learning Space**—Work with your catechetical leader or parish staff to make sure that Bibles are available for use in your learning space. Ideally, all of your participants should have access to a Catholic Bible each time you gather.

5. **Use the Bible Regularly in Your Sessions**—Don't limit the Bible to prayer. Feel free to bring in a Bible story at any time during your lesson to further illustrate the point of your lesson. When your textbook refers to a Bible passage, set the textbook aside for a moment and have your participants locate the passage in the Bible. In doing so, your participants will gradually develop familiarity with the Bible. Have one of the participants read the passage aloud from the enthroned Bible in your prayer space.

> According to *Life* magazine, the single most important event in the second Christian millennium was "Gutenberg prints the Bible."

6. **Bring the Bible Stories to Life**—Select stories and passages that can be either proclaimed creatively, dramatized, role-played, drawn, or viewed on video. It is important that participants, especially children, see or hear these stories come to life so that they can begin making connections to their own life experiences and circumstances. If Bible stories are indeed to provide us with a vision, it is helpful to be able to see them and not just listen to them.

7. **Use the Lectionary as a Guide**—If you are having trouble figuring out where to go to select Bible stories, use the guide that the church provides: the cycle of readings in the Lectionary. You can use a resource such as "Sunday Connection" at www.FindingGod.org to prepare your participants for the readings they will hear at Mass the following Sunday. These readings will help your participants become more familiar not only with the Bible but also with the church's liturgical cycle.

> "The Holy Bible is like a mirror before our mind's eye. In it we see our inner face. From the Scriptures we can learn our spiritual deformities and beauties. And there too we discover the progress we are making and how far we are from perfection."
> —POPE ST. GREGORY THE GREAT

8. **Teach Bible Skills**—Help your participants to become more proficient in using the Bible. Teach them how to use Biblical citation (1 Pt 2:3–4 represents the First Letter of Peter, chapter 2, verses 3 through 4). Demonstrate how to use the table of contents in the Bible to locate books. Have your learners partici-pate in Bible searches by locating passages in the Bible and sum-marizing what they find. In sum-mary, make sure that the Bible is a familiar tool for your participants to turn to in their faith formation.

Glossary

Fundamentalism—Some Christians believe that because the Bible is the inspired word of God, every passage must be interpreted literally. This approach, called fundamentalism, does not distinguish between truth and fact. A fundamentalist would say that if the Bible tells us that Jonah was swallowed by a large fish, then it literally happened. This approach to interpreting the Bible is fraught with problems that limit the reader's abil-ity to apply the truths to contemporary experience. Catholics also believe in the Bible's inerrancy, but in relation to religious truth—not necessarily historical and scientific information. In other words, the story of Jonah and the large fish teaches us divine truths, without error, about our rela-tionship with God. This is regardless of scientific truths about the pos-sibility of a man living in the belly of a large fish for three days.

Contextualism—Catholics do not use a fundamentalist approach to the Bible but rather a contextualist approach. A contextualist approach attempts to look at the whole passage in context and determine what meaning or truth is being conveyed to the reader beyond the facts of the story. Thus, a contextualist would not be as concerned with the issue of whether Jonah was factually swallowed by a large fish but with the truth being conveyed in the story: running from God's will is futile and can be likened to being swallowed up in the darkness.

Troubleshooting

Are you trying to find something in the Bible but can't? Do you feel lost? Confused? Don't give up. Here are several tips.

➕ **First, get a hold of a Bible concordance (see if your catechetical leader has one or can acquire one).** A Bible concordance is a reference book that assists you in locating passages, people, themes, and events in the Bible. It also provides background on topics to help you understand them better.

➕ **Second, become familiar with the table of contents of your Bible.** Learn the abbreviations to books of the Bible, or at least know what page the abbreviations can be found on in your Bible's table of contents. Your familiarity with the Bible's table of contents will save you a great deal of time when you attempt to locate passages.

➕ **Finally, become familiar with the proper citation used for biblical passages: book, chapter, and verse.** Some of us may be intimidated when confronted with a citation such as 1 Kgs 3:1–7, 9. Using your table of contents, you will find the abbreviation to be: the First Book of Kings, chapter 3, verses 1 through 7, and verse 9. Your table of contents will then help you locate the page number.

Scripture

"But you, remain faithful to what you have learned and believed, because you know from whom you learned it, and that from infancy you have known [the] sacred scriptures, which are capable of giving you wisdom for salvation through faith in Christ Jesus. All scripture is inspired by God and is useful for teaching, for refutation, for correction, and for training in righteousness."

(2 TIMOTHY 3:14–16)

Prayer

Help me, Lord, to better know you through the stories of Scripture so that I may be filled with your wisdom. Guide me in using the stories and illustrations of Scripture in my lessons so that those I teach will be trained in righteousness and will learn the way that leads to salvation.

For an opportunity to companion with other catechists and to nourish our vocation, visit www.catechistsjourney.com.

Chapter Fourteen

Power Tools:
Using Technology

Over the past few decades, things have really changed in the world of home repair. Today, power tools are available for almost any task: driving a nail, sinking a screw, sanding a piece of wood, drilling a hole, or even painting a wall. The trick, of course, is to make sure that you know how to use the power tools properly so that they really do complete your repairs in less time and with greater efficiency. While power tools have changed the world of home improvement, one thing has not changed: the work needs to be done with attention to detail and commitment to quality.

> **"In addition to the numerous traditional means used in catechesis, all the various instruments of the mass media should be employed to proclaim the Gospel message."**
>
> *NATIONAL DIRECTORY FOR CATECHESIS*, 30

Using Technology: Power Tools for the Effective Catechist

One day, when I was teaching religion in a high school, I entered the audiovisual room and was met with a flurry of activity as students assisted the librarian in preparing to deliver AV equipment to classrooms. The librarian took a deep breath, looked over at me, and said, "What did Aquinas and Augustine do without AV equipment?"

It's true that for centuries the church's greatest teachers accomplished wonderful things without the assistance of a kilowatt of electricity. By the same token, they used whatever was the state of the art for their day. As literacy became more and more widespread, the written word came to be just as crucial as the spoken word, which once seemed sufficient. Today, young people rely on computers in the primary grades, where storybooks once seemed sufficient. Young people today are accustomed to being engaged, if not entertained, by video images and audio sounds throughout their day. It only makes sense that those of us in catechesis attempt to utilize the tools that are available today to reach our participants in the most effective manner.

> A child was watching his mother sift through and delete a long list of junk e-mail on the computer screen.
>
> "This reminds me of the Lord's Prayer," the child said.
>
> "What do you mean?" the mother asked.
>
> "You know. That part about 'deliver us from e-mail.'"

Skills, Tips, and Practical Advice for Effective Use of Technology

Let's take a look at how we can most effectively use technology in our learning environment to enhance our lessons.

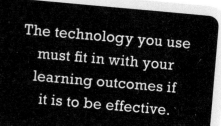

1. **Decide on the Most Effective Medium for Your Lesson—** The technology you use must fit in with your learning outcomes if it is to be effective. If your learning outcomes call for engaging participants in an experience of sharing and articulating, then it may not be the right time to show a video that will make them passive. Remember that technology is a tool to help you achieve a goal. One does not use a power drill to sand a piece of wood. Be sure your selection of technology will help you achieve your lesson's learning outcomes.

2. **Familiarize Yourself with the Equipment—**Be sure to take the time to look over the equipment you are going to use in order to familiarize yourself with its features and directions for proper use. Also, when it comes to technology, if you are in doubt about how something works,

ask a child or teenager for help. Chances are that one or more of your participants is adept at using the equipment that is mystifying you. Arrange for this participant to be your technology assistant.

3. **Do a Test Run on Your Presentation**—Familiarize yourself with how to change the volume and brightness, and work the play, stop, and pause features. Consider placing a bright sticker on the buttons you need to use in order to find them quickly during the lesson (especially if the lights are dimmed for a reflective mood). In addition, running a test on the equipment will help you make sure all of the bugs have been worked out.

4. **Don't Trust Technology Just Because It's Technology**—Most of us tend to have a blind trust for technology. We assume that our equipment is going to work just because it is a product of modern technology. Don't fall into this trap. Numerous problems can arise when using technology if we trust the equipment so implicitly that we don't think it necessary to check it out ahead of time.

5. **Preview Your Materials**—Be sure to preview any material, such as video or music clips, that you are going to use in your session. Your DVD may not be good quality. Your transparency may be upside down or may contain spelling mistakes. Your music CD may have objectionable lyrics. The bottom line is, don't spend so much time inspecting the equipment that you ignore the material you will be using it with.

> **When it comes to technology, if you are in doubt about how something works, ask a child or teenager for help.**

The director of religious education led the catechists in prayer, offering her petitions at the top of her lungs.

"Lord, we pray for a new DVD player for our program!"

One of the catechists leaned over and said, "Why are you shouting? God is not hard of hearing."

The DRE replied, "No, but the business manager is!"

6. **"Line-Up" Your Tape, CD, DVD, or Videotape**—Few things can frustrate a catechist more than attempting to play a song or video clip only to find that the tape, CD, or DVD is not set to the right spot. The time it takes to locate the correct spot can seem like an eternity when done in front of others, and can result in loss of control of your group. It is important to have your material "lined up" to the spot you intend to play.

7. **Practice Shutting Off Equipment**—The inability to turn equipment *off* can be just as frustrating as the inability to turn equipment *on*. Allowing a video or song to play beyond its intended ending can ruin the mood you had hoped to set. By the same token, it is always a good idea to slowly fade the volume before pressing Stop on any piece of equipment. I've seen many prayerful moods destroyed by catechists who hit a Stop button in the middle of a song or video clip because it was time to move on. The resulting "explosion" of static or abrupt silence can be disconcerting to the group that was engaged by the viewing or listening.

> The inability to turn equipment *off* can be just as frustrating as the inability to turn equipment *on*.

8. **Technology Is a Means to an End**—It is not an end in and of itself. To get the most effective use of your technology, provide your participants with an introduction and overview of anything they are about to see or listen to. Likewise, direct your participants to focus on something specific while they are viewing or listening so that they can be active learners instead of passive observers. Instruct your participants to pay attention to certain details and have them jot down notes on a worksheet as they watch or listen. When the viewing or listening is over, process what you have shown or played and integrate it into the lesson.

> "[T]he Church takes advantage of the opportunities offered by the communications media as pathways providentially given by God to intensify communion and to render more penetrating the proclamation of His word."
> —POPE JOHN PAUL II, THE RAPID DEVELOPMENT OF TECHNOLOGY (6)

DVD/VCR—Today, digital video disc (DVD) players are as common in most homes as transistor radios were decades ago. DVDs allow you to conveniently locate scenes without waiting for a fast-forward or rewind function to complete. Videocassette recorders, although still a reliable medium, are fast becoming obsolete.

Projection TV—A projection TV allows you to show a video or a TV program to a larger group of participants on a large screen as though in a small movie theater. A projection TV simply projects the image from a TV/VCR/DVD player onto a large screen for viewing by a larger audience.

PowerPoint Presentation—PowerPoint is a graphics program by Microsoft that allows you to produce a professional-looking presentation made up of a series of "slides." The slide presentation, which can contain graphics and images, is prepared on your computer and then, through an LCD projector, is projected onto a screen. This type of slide presentation can be useful for providing an outline and highlights of your lesson as a visual aid. Likewise, you can design a meditation using a PowerPoint presentation, inviting your participants to reflect on inspirational images set to reflective music.

A SMART Board—A SMART Board is a large interactive whiteboard that is touch sensitive, giving you "fingertip" control of the information on your computer that is being projected onto the board. You can control the computer by touching the board either directly or with a special pen. In other words, your finger acts as a mouse while the special pen writes in digital "ink" on the screen. Any notes that you write on the board can be converted to typed text and saved to the computer.

The World Wide Web—The World Wide Web and the Internet provide you and your learners with almost unlimited access to information, resources, and ideas that can serve your lessons. Consider the following:

a. Be extraordinarily careful about sending your participants to surf the Internet for information.
b. Make sure you have researched any Web sites you want them to visit to ensure that the information is acceptable.
c. When working with children, make sure parents are aware of any Internet assignments you have given.

d. If your parish has a Web site, you may be able to provide a link for your participants and/or their parents so that they can access information and activities related to your lessons outside of class time. By providing these materials online, you provide your participants with increased flexibility and opportunities for learning.

e. The Internet also provides you, as a catechist, with access to quality Catholic information and resources.

f. Most likely, the publisher of your textbook hosts a Web site where you can go for additional information and resources. (For a sample, visit www.FindingGod.org.)

A catechist was showing children how to use the Internet to find Catholic Web sites about the Bible. She noticed that when one of the children attempted to log onto a Bible Web site, he used a very long password. She asked him what it was and he replied, "ZacchaeusLazarusPontiusPilateMaryMagdalene." She asked him why he would use such a password. "Because," he explained, "it says your password has to have at least four characters."

g. Also, your diocese most likely has a Web site with links to other quality Catholic sites.

h. Be aware of the fact that many Web sites using the name *Catholic* are not necessarily reliable or authentically Catholic. (For a list of reliable Catholic Web sites, see Appendix 2 of this book.)

Pope John Paul II referred to the mass media, including the Internet, as the "first Areopagus of the modern age" (*Redemptoris missio*, 37c). The Areopagus was a public meeting place in ancient Athens where ideas could be freely expressed, exchanged, and debated.

LCD Projector—A projection device that combines three liquid crystal display panels (hence LCD) and a high intensity light source to project images from a computer onto a screen for a presentation. LCD projectors are used for PowerPoint presentations (as described on page 105), and can also be linked to video cameras to project images onto a screen.

"You can't just punch in 'let there be light' without writing the code underlying the user interface functions."

Overhead Projector—An overhead projector is basically an electronic chalkboard. It produces an image by transmitting light through a transparency lying on the face of the projector. A lens and mirror arrangement then projects the image onto a screen. You can effectively utilize transparencies to illustrate or outline important points for a lesson without ever having to turn your back on your group to write on the board. You can prepare transparencies ahead of time or write on them during your session with dry-erase markers. Thus, you are using an electronic chalkboard. Participants are easily engaged by use of an overhead, because the lights go off and their focus is easily fixed on the large bright image. Attempt to prepare transparencies ahead of time for best use, and always have an extra projection bulb on hand in case one burns out.

CD/Cassette Player—Today, CDs have replaced vinyl records and, for the most part, cassette tapes. A CD is a compact disc that plays music by result of a laser, instead of a needle or tape head. The clarity of a CD is far superior to that of an audiocassette. A CD can provide some excellent sounds for prayer experiences. Both CD and audio cassette players work much the same way with simple On/Off, Play, Pause, Forward, Rewind, and Stop buttons. With CDs, it is easier to locate a song on the disc because of the track selection features.

MP3 Player—Another source for playing music is an MP3 player, which allows you to download music (as compressed digital audio files) from the Internet. Usually intended for personal use, an MP3 player may be docked to an amplifier to play to a group.

Troubleshooting

➕ When technology glitches pop up, make sure you know whom you can call on (DRE, principal, maintenance person, colleague, reliable participant, etc.) to come to the rescue.

➕ Check on the visibility/audibility of your presentation. Nothing is worse than starting a video or tape/CD only to realize that a majority of your group cannot see or hear it. Part of your preparation should be to make sure that every seat "in the house" is good.

➕ Most problems using technology can easily be avoided by proper preparation and familiarization with the tools you are using. Power buttons, cords, Play/Stop buttons, volume switches, etc., rarely cause trouble unless we are using them improperly. Minimize these problems by doing your homework before your session.

➕ Videos sold for educational purposes can be used freely in educational settings. All other videos have copyright restrictions. If you want to use them in an educational setting, your school or parish must have a yearly license. For more information on this, visit the Web site of Movie Licensing USA (www.movlic.com).

Scripture

"The churches of Asia send you greetings. Aquila and Prisca together with the church at their house send you many greetings in the Lord. All the brothers greet you. Greet one another with a holy kiss. I, Paul, write this greeting in my own hand."

(1 CORINTHIANS 16:19–21)

Prayer

St. Paul was the first to use the medium of the letter to spread the gospel of Jesus. Today, there are so many tools available to use in preaching your word, Lord. Help me to be as innovative as St. Paul was. Help me to best utilize technology in my lessons so that I may capture the imagination of my participants and bring the power of your word to life.

For an opportunity to companion with other catechists and to nourish our vocation, visit www.catechistsjourney.com.

Chapter Fifteen

Scrapers: Using Questions to Get beneath the Surface

When my wife and I bought our first house, we were impressed mainly with its potential. After we moved in, the work began. Every room and every wall was to be painted or wallpapered. This was easier said than done. What I thought was going to be an easy "peeling off" job became a project for my scraper and my elbows. Bit by bit, I scraped off the old wallpaper that stubbornly held onto the wall. It took a great deal of effort, but, eventually, I was able to get down to the smooth natural surface of the wall and begin the fun task of putting up the new wallpaper or paint. The result was tremendous. The little house that we thought had so much potential lived up to our dream.

Asking Questions to Get beneath the Surface

Those we teach are so full of potential. We just need to know how to get beneath the surface or exterior that sometimes seems to cover up that potential. As catechists, one of the most effective ways we do this is by using the tool of *asking questions*. Jesus was, of course, a master at this skill. Often in the Gospels, we find Jesus utilizing questions to challenge his followers and stimulate their thinking. As catechists, we too need to utilize questions in our lessons so that we may get beneath the surface of our participants and tap the rich potential that lies inside of them.

> "Jesus . . . engaged them (his apostles) in lively conversations by asking them probing questions: 'Who do people say that I am?'"
>
> *National Directory for Catechesis*, 28A-2

★ ★

The following are some of the questions that Jesus asked:

★ "But who do you say that I am?"
(Mark 8:29)

★ "Whose image is this and whose inscription?" (Matthew 22:20)

★ "Did you not know that I must be in my Father's house?" (Luke 2:49)

★ "Which is easier, to say, 'Your sins are forgiven,' or to say, 'Rise and walk'?" (Luke 5:23)

★ "Can the wedding guests fast while the bridegroom is with them?" (Mark 2:19)

★ "Which of these three, in your opinion, was neighbor to the robbers' victim?" (Luke 10:36)

★ ★

Skills, Tips, and Practical Advice for Asking Questions

One of Jesus' most famous sayings refers to the act of asking a question: "Ask and it will be given to you" (Matthew 7:7). I have come to believe that our task as catechists is not so much to provide answers for our participants, but to teach them to ask the right questions in their lives. When they ask, they shall receive. Let's take a look at the proper use of questions in our lessons.

1. **Phrase Your Questions in a Simple, Straightforward Way**—Avoid complicated questions that turn and twist so much that participants can't figure out what you're really looking for. Keep the question short and to the point.

2. **Keep Your Questions Open-Ended**—Avoid asking questions that will result in a yes or no response. An open-ended question is one that invites the participants to dig a little deeper and express some thoughts, insights, and opinions of their own. For example, instead of asking "Did Jesus ever show any feelings or emotions?" you would ask, "When were some times that Jesus showed some feelings or emotions?"

3. **Don't Answer Your Own Questions**—All too often, catechists panic when no one volunteers to answer a question. To save face, they answer the question themselves. Remember our chapter on the spotlight? When you ask a question, you have placed the focus on the participants. Keep it there. Be patient. Give the participants time to think. If they're having trouble answering, try rephrasing the question.

> An open-ended question is one that invites the participants to dig a little deeper and express some thoughts, insights, and opinions of their own.

4. **Ask a Question and Then Repeat It**—Asking a question once is never enough. Get in the habit of asking a question, pausing, and then asking the question again in exactly the same way. Do this even if a hand shoots up after the first time. By pausing and repeating the question, you give participants that may be slower to respond an opportunity to jump in.

5. **As You Await an Answer, Move around the Room and Make Eye Contact**—As you ask and repeat a question, move around the room and make eye contact with participants. This is a way of communicating to them that you expect an answer and will patiently wait until you get one.

6. **Ask a Question of the Whole Group First**—Whenever you ask a question, direct it to the whole group first. If you single out one participant, the rest of the group will relax, thinking that they're off the hook. Occasionally, you may need to single out someone whose attention is wavering, but the whole group should have the opportunity to respond.

7. **Plan Your Questions ahead of Time**—Your catechist manual most likely offers questions for discussion. Look these over ahead of time to make sure they will serve your purposes. Don't hesitate to prepare additional questions. Write out your questions ahead of time so that you don't go blank when you need them. Shorten and rephrase them until you feel they will achieve their goal most effectively.

8. **Give Feedback to Participants When They Respond to Questions—** If a participant answers a question and you do not acknowledge the answer, he or she may feel ignored or unappreciated. Learners participate more if they feel that their contributions are appreciated. Be sure to tell participants "That's excellent," or "You make a very good point." Even if a participant answers incorrectly, do not embarrass him or her by saying, "No, you're wrong." Instead, say something such as, "Nice try—let's see if someone can help you."

9. **Leading Discussion—**Asking questions in your lessons is part of the larger context of leading discussions. Discussions are an important means of assessing participants' understanding of a topic. Discussions promote active engagement in learning and allow participants an opportunity to express themselves.

Tips for Leading Discussions

- Ask questions that go beyond retrieving information and invite individual's thoughts, opinions, and feelings.
- Invite more than one response to a question.
- Ask for reactions to previous responses.
- Occasionally, summarize what you heard and invite more discussion.
- Encourage respectful listening.
- Assure confidentiality.

Glossary

Questions come in two basic categories: *impersonal* and *personal*. Each of these categories can be further broken down into two smaller categories: informational/implicational and individual/ideological. The four *Is* (as I refer to them) describe the type of answer the questioner is looking for. Like peeling away layers of an onion, each category delves deeper into the heart of the responder.

"The important thing is not to stop questioning."
—Albert Einstein

Impersonal

Informational—These questions skim the surface and are very nonthreatening. Asking an informational question is a great way to begin a discussion. For example, "What is another name for Jesus' Sermon on the Mount?" The answer is strictly informational: "The Beatitudes."

Implicational—These questions go beneath the surface in search of significance. For example, "What is Jesus trying to tell us in the Beatitudes?" The response is beyond informational but does not require the responder to reveal anything personal.

"I still don't have all the answers, but I'm beginning to ask the right questions."

Personal

Individual—These questions delve into the thoughts, opinions, and feelings of the individual responding. For example, "How can *you* try to live out the Beatitudes in your life?" Obviously, this type of question can seem threatening because more is being revealed. On the other hand, it leads to a much more meaningful and enjoyable discussion.

Ideological—These questions invite participants to speculate and to grapple with deep issues rather than to give right or wrong answers. For example, "What do you think the world would look like if everyone lived the Beatitudes?" To respond on this level is to reveal one's personal thoughts, hopes, and dreams.

A Sunday school teacher asked her class, "Does anyone here know what we mean by sins of omission?"

A small girl replied, "Aren't those the sins we should have committed, but didn't?"

Troubleshooting

Few things can bring about more silence in a room than a question being asked. Rather than growing nervous about the silence, relish the fact that you have engaged the partici-pants. The silence reflects the fact that they are thinking. Be patient and repeat the question. You may rephrase the question if necessary, but resist the temptation to answer it yourself. Sooner or later an answer will come. Ask and you shall receive.

"If you don't ask, you don't get."
—Mahatma Gandhi

Scripture

"Then the disciples of John approached him and said, 'Why do we and the Pharisees fast [much], but your disciples do not fast?' Jesus answered them, 'Can the wedding guests mourn as long as the bridegroom is with them?'"

(Matthew 9:14–15)

Prayer

Jesus, you knew how to ask questions of your followers in order to help them come to understand the truth. Help me to ask questions of my participants that will get beneath the surface and delve into their hearts. Help me to unlock their true potential so that the power of your Spirit may be unleashed. Help me to use questions as if I was scraping away old paint or wallpaper, revealing the true beauty of each participant in the process. Help me to teach them to ask the right questions of life; thus, its mysteries will slowly and gradually be revealed to them and they will come to recognize time and again that *you* are the answer they are seeking.

For an opportunity to companion with other catechists and to nourish our vocation, visit www.catechistsjourney.com.

The Catechist's Toolbox

Chapter Sixteen

Tape Measures: Assessing Progress

Carpenters teach their apprentices the following phrase: "measure twice, cut once." I wish someone had taught me that before I attempted to put up wall paneling in my basement. Sure, I had a tape measure, but I wasn't measuring as accurately as I needed to. As a result, I ended up wasting a lot of paneling. In order to do effective home improvement, you need to take accurate measurements.

> "Diocesan catechetical offices should . . . provide assistance in the evaluation of parish catechetical programs, using instruments that measure cognitive, affective, and behavioral objectives."
>
> *NATIONAL DIRECTORY FOR CATECHESIS,* 59c

Assessing (Measuring) Faith Formation

In catechesis, we are constantly assessing whether or not learners are grasping a way of life.

How do we measure effectiveness in catechesis? How do we know whether or not we have achieved our learning outcomes? We may feel as though we've had a very good session. One catechist I know judges success on whether or not the participants had fun. That's not a very reliable method of assessing whether or not someone has been further equipped to live as a disciple of Jesus. In catechesis, we are constantly assessing whether or not learners are grasping a way of life. That means more than simply giving a quiz or test to determine if participants can recall certain concepts.

Jesus was constantly assessing the growth of his disciples.

★ On numerous occasions, after preaching a parable, Jesus asked his followers if they understood its meaning.

★ The Gospels of Matthew, Mark, and Luke tell us that Jesus asked his disciples, "Who do you say that I am?" *(Mark 8:29)* as he attempted to assess their understanding of his identity.

★ At the Last Supper, after he had washed the feet of the apostles, he sat back down and asked them, "Do you realize what I have done for you?" *(John 13:12).*

If we are to teach as Jesus did, we must constantly be assessing—in a variety of forms—whether his present-day followers are grasping the knowledge and skills needed to be a disciple in today's world.

Skills, Tips, and Practical Advice for Doing Assessment in Catechesis

Assessment (from the Latin *assidere* meaning "to sit with") is something we do *with* and *for* a learner, not *to* a learner. We are not only assessing *their* comprehension of key concepts but also *our* effectiveness in transmitting those concepts. We seek to assess the formation that is taking place in our learners and offer feedback leading to further growth. Since people learn in a variety of ways, a variety of forms of assessment are needed. In catechesis, assessment takes on many forms.

> Assessment (from the Latin *assidere* meaning "to sit with") is something we do with and *for* a learner, not *to* a learner.

1. **Doing Formal Assessment**—A formal assessment asks the question: What do you know and understand? This type of assessment, accomplished in either written or oral forms, models Jesus' attempts to assess his disciples' understanding of his teaching and actions. When using quizzes or tests, keep the following in mind:

A formal assessment asks the question: What do you know and understand?

> Make sure that the items included on your quizzes or tests are consistent with the learning outcomes for your lesson.
> Provide your learners with opportunities for self-assessment. In other words, ask them to express whether or not they feel that they comprehend what's being taught. Also ask them to identify concepts that they are having difficulty with.
> Provide prompt feedback on quizzes and tests.
> Remember that, in catechesis, assessments are not intended to determine a grade but to indicate which concepts (or individuals) need further attention.

A catechist was giving a true/false quiz. He was strolling around the room, surveying the students at work. He came upon one student who was flipping a coin and then writing. He asked, "What are you doing?" The student replied, "Getting the answers to the quiz." The catechist shook his head and walked on. A little while later, when everyone was finished with the quiz, the catechist noticed the student was again flipping the coin. He asked, "Now what are you doing?" The student responded, "I'm checking the answers."

Become Familiar with ACRE and IFG—The Assessment of Catechesis/Religious Education (ACRE), provided by the National Catholic Education Association (NCEA), is a formal assessment tool used to assist Catholic schools, religious education programs, and dioceses in evaluating the faith knowledge and attitudes of young people in the following areas:

◆ God

◆ Church

◆ Liturgy and Sacraments

◆ Revelation (Scripture and Faith)

◆ Morality and Catholic Social Teaching

◆ Church History

◆ Prayer/Religious Practices

◆ Catholic Literacy

ACRE is designed to be used with young people on three levels: level one (fifth grade); level two (eighth or ninth grade); and level three (eleventh or twelfth grade). ACRE is not used to assess individuals, but rather to evaluate the effectiveness of a catechetical program as a whole. Each site that uses ACRE receives a group report that includes an analysis of participants' responses. Individuals who wish to may receive a student report on the faith knowledge section of the assessment.

The Information for Growth (IFG) survey can assist adults in assessing their faith knowledge and spiritual growth. Group reports are also provided, again, to assist the parish in evaluating the effectiveness of adult catechesis.

By using ACRE or IFG, parishes are able to assess the extent to which learners are grasping concepts of our faith tradition and make changes in their curriculum accordingly.

2. **Doing Informal Assessment**—Informal assessment asks What can you do with what you know, and how do you do it?

> Informal assessment asks: What can you do with what you know, and how do you do it?

- ◆ **Ongoing**—Include opportunities to assess your participants' grasp of concepts by observing their participation in discussions, group work, prayer/reflection, and service to others.

- ◆ **Specific Tasks**—Include specific opportunities to evaluate verbal (oral and written) and nonverbal (drawn, crafted, etc.) expressions and responses. These need not be quizzes or tests but may simply be activities that invite your participants to express (in a variety of forms) their understanding or application of various concepts.

3. **Authentic Assessment**—Authentic assessment is exactly what the name implies—genuine and real. Authentic assessment is performance based: learners put into action what they've been learning about. Beyond being able to speak or write about what it means to be a disciple of Jesus, learners must have opportunities to live out the call to discipleship.

- ◆ **Service Experiences**—Provide suggestions for specific ways that your learners can put their faith into practice by serving others, either individually or as a group.

- ◆ **Participant Portfolios**—A portfolio is a collection of a learner's work over time. Portfolios are a means for allowing learners to see their growth and progress. Portfolios also give catechists the opportunity to gain insight into their participants' efforts, progress, achievements, and thought processes, as well as their strengths and needs. One of the advantages of using portfolios is that learners are actively engaged in their own ongoing assessment. However, catechists need to help learners identify portfolio-worthy assignments (see sidebar on page 120). File folders or binders can be used as portfolios because it is easy for learners to add or take work out of them over time. Learners should have easy access to their portfolios and should be encouraged to interact with their portfolios often.

Tape Measures: Assessing Progress

Here are some suggestions for portfolio-worthy assignments that might be included in a catechetical portfolio.

◆ Written reflections on Scripture passages

◆ Prayers composed by the participant

◆ Traditional prayers taken to heart (memorized)

◆ Tear-out pages from their student text showing work completed

◆ Formal assessments taken (tests and quizzes)

◆ Written reflections on faith-building experiences (retreats, service experiences, worship or prayer experiences, etc.)

◆ Projects such as drawings of Scripture stories or saints, designs for a parish bulletin, a version of a contemporary parable, a collage of pictures showing Catholic social teaching themes in action, a Lenten calendar showing Lenten promises, a homemade rosary, or research on a saint

> **A student's prayer: "Now I lay me down to rest, and hope to pass tomorrow's test. If I should die before I wake, that's one less test I have to take."**

◆ "Faith Surveys" where learners assess the extent of their participation in Catholic practices (something that could be done at the beginning and end of a year or at the end of each year a participant is in a catechetical program)

4. **Pay Attention to Various Learning Styles**—Any approach to assessment would be incomplete without an understanding of the various ways that people learn. Refer to chapter 5 in this book for a better understanding of the many ways that your participants can express their grasp of the concepts you are presenting.

Troubleshooting

Assessment is often wrongly equated with testing in order to determine a grade. In catechesis, testing is only one form of assessing learners' readiness to live as disciples of Jesus Christ. Catechists, like most people, are eager for tangible results from their work. The temptation can be to reduce catechesis to "learning your catechism," meaning that the learner simply needs to show that he or she has memorized a set of cognitive principles. (If this were the case, we wouldn't need catechists. We could just hand out little catechisms and have people memorize them.) Although there is certainly a place in catechesis for giving quizzes and tests to determine whether key concepts are being grasped, assessment must also include a variety of methods that will enable you to determine how successfully participants are learning to live the Catholic way of life.

The temptation can be to reduce catechesis to "learning your catechism," meaning that the learner simply needs to show that he or she has memorized a set of cognitive principles.

Glossary

In general, assessment takes three forms: **formal assessment** (quizzes, tests, essays); **informal assessment** (observation of learners' grasp of concepts by observing their participation in written work, group work, and group activities); and **authentic assessment** (providing opportunities for participants to put into action what they've been learning).

"I'd like you to excel."

Tape Measures: Assessing Progress

Scripture

"So when he had washed their feet [and] put his garments back on and reclined at table again, he said to them, 'Do you realize what I have done for you?'"

(JOHN 13:12)

Prayer

Lord Jesus, when you washed the feet of your disciples, you asked them if they understood what you had just done for them. You taught and then you assessed the extent to which your message penetrated. Help me to teach your word and to assess the effectiveness of my efforts so that I might know how to better invite my participants to learn the way of salvation.

For an opportunity to companion with other catechists and to nourish our vocation, visit www.catechistsjourney.com.

Chapter Seventeen

Apprenticeship: Teaching and Learning by Doing

My father was a pharmacist, and the only tools I ever saw him use were a mortar and pestle. I never saw him paint, hammer, saw, or drill. Needless to say, I was apprenticed in the ways of running a retail pharmacy but not in the ways of home repairs.

> "Learning by apprenticeship is . . . an important human element in catechetical methodology."
>
> *National Directory for Catechesis,* 29H

When our family business was forced to move into a new storefront that was badly in need of redecorating and repairs, I volunteered to take on the painting, the wallpapering, and the installation of a new floor. Only one problem stood in the way—I didn't know how to do any of these things. Luckily for me, my brother-in-law was quite handy with tools and home repairs, and stepped forward to lend his expertise. Over the next few weeks, I learned more about home repairs than I had in my whole life because I was properly apprenticed by someone who knew how to show me the tricks of the trade.

It's All in the Doing

An ancient proverb says that "to know, and not to do, is really not to know." As catechists, we can attend all kinds of workshops and read all kinds of books (like this one) and come to the conclusion that we really know how to be an effective catechist. However, the only real teacher in life is experience. It is in the *doing* of catechesis that we grow and develop in our ministry. By the same token, it is only when our participants become involved in doing the work of the gospel that they truly learn the gospel. Let's take a look at how we, as catechists, can learn by doing and how we in turn can teach more effectively by apprenticing our participants.

Step-by-Step Instructions for Apprenticing

FOR OURSELVES:

1. **Try New Things**—One definition of insanity is this: doing the same thing over and over again while expecting different results. If we are dissatisfied with the effectiveness of our lessons and would like to achieve different results, we cannot continue to teach the same way. Part of being an apprentice is having the opportunity to try out new skills under the supervision of a mentor. Think of yourself as an apprentice (no matter how long you've been teaching), and try something new in your lessons in hopes of bringing about new results.

2. **Get a Mentor**—It is important that you maintain communication with a mentor—someone who can provide you with the insight you need to hone your skills and continue acquiring new ones. A mentor can be your director of religious education, a fellow catechist or Catholic schoolteacher, a principal, a parent, or even a teacher who once taught you. Seek out a veteran catechist whose "toolbox" is loaded with teaching tools, skills, and ideas that you would love to acquire. By the same token, if you're a veteran catechist, seek out new catechists to see what kinds of fresh, creative, and energetic ideas they are bringing to their lessons these days.

> "Mentor: Someone whose hindsight can become your foresight."
> —Anonymous

3. **Accept New Challenges**—Years after completing my master's degree in pastoral studies and shortly after finishing my doctor of ministry degree, I took on an even greater challenge: I became a catechist for eighth graders! After many years away from the classroom, the experience of teaching junior high was both exciting and challenging. As a catechist, don't be afraid of challenges that come your way. You may be asked to take on a new subject or a new age group.

> 66 Start by doing what's necessary; then do what's possible; and suddenly you are doing the impossible. 99
> —St. Francis of Assisi

You may also be asked to become a leader of prayer, a liturgical minister for children's liturgies, an RCIA catechist, or a leader of Scripture study. Don't shy away from these challenges. Accept them and find a mentor who will assist you in developing in this new area you are venturing into.

> Excellence goes hand in hand with the ability to make adjustments. Wisdom is the result of mistakes reflected upon.

4. **Learn from Your Mistakes**—Apprentices make mistakes. You will make mistakes. After a quarter of a century of ministry experience, I still make mistakes. The difference between an effective catechist and one who is not effective is the ability to learn from those mistakes. If things go wrong in your lesson, don't say, "Never again." Instead, ask yourself, "How will I do this differently next time?" because there *will* be a next time. Excellence goes hand in hand with the ability to make adjustments. Wisdom is the result of mistakes reflected upon.

My Bad

As a young catechist, I once led a prayer service for teens that resulted in a young man coming to tears in front of everyone. I was embarrassed for him and told everyone we would take a break. Then I led him out of the room to let him compose himself. The associate pastor (my mentor) later told me that I had no reason to lead that young man out of the room. His tears were his prayer. I could have comforted him and affirmed his sharing of emotion. I felt terrible that I had communicated to this young man that crying was something to be ashamed of. Instead of staying away from emotional prayer experiences, I vowed to change the way I reacted to tears. Since that time, I have had many people, young and old, cry in the presence of others while at prayer. I have learned to quietly comfort someone who is crying, often just by placing a hand on his or her shoulder, and thanking that person for sharing his or her tears with the group. From my mistake, I learned to become a better catechist and have helped others to express themselves in whatever way the Spirit has moved them.

1. **Become a Mentor**—As a catechist, your job is not to become friends with your learners but to become a mentor to them. Think of your participants as apprentices who have been entrusted to you to learn the skills they will need to live the Christian life. Like a good coach who lets the players play the game, a good catechist learns how to teach "from the sidelines." This allows participants to put skills and ideas to work while you offer them guidance and support.

> Our participants are not sponges waiting to soak up our wisdom. They are apprentices waiting to be shown how to use the skills we were once taught.

2. **Let Go**—As catechists, we sometimes think that if something is going to get done, we have to do it ourselves. Wrong. The effective catechist knows how to share the work with his or her participants, and in doing so, he or she apprentices them. Show participants how to take attendance, write on the board for you, distribute and collect books and papers, lead prayer, and even lead discussion. Our participants are not sponges waiting to soak up our wisdom. They are apprentices waiting to be shown how to use the skills we were once taught.

3. **Follow the Example of John the Baptist**—John the Baptist once said, "He must increase; I must decrease" (John 3:30). This is the prayer of a mentor. John knew when it was time for him to step aside and allow Jesus to take over the spotlight. As catechists, we, too, need to step aside and allow our participants to reach their potential by allowing them to do the work of the gospel while we mentor them.

4. **Think "Laboratory" and "Field Trips"**—A laboratory is a place where experiments are conducted. Our learning space is just that: a laboratory where our apprentices experiment with the gospel message of Jesus and test it out before putting it into practice in the real world. Practice employing a "field trip" mentality that challenges your participants to apply new knowledge and skills in real-life situations. For example, if you are talking about love of enemies or turning the

other cheek, give your participants an assignment that will require them to perform some action that applies these principles. Later, discuss the successes and failures that were encountered, knowing that you have just apprenticed your participants in the gospel of Jesus. Likewise, consider specific ways that participants can put their faith into practice serving others, either individually or as a group.

5. **Implement Catholic Social Teaching**—The Catholic Church has a long tradition of applying the gospel to various situations in society in order that society may be transformed. We call this tradition Catholic social teaching. One of the most profound ways of apprenticing participants into the Catholic way of life is to engage them in experiences that put Catholic social teaching into action. Here is an overview of the principles of Catholic social teaching as outlined by the United States Conference of Catholic Bishops.

> If you are talking about love of enemies or turning the other cheek, give your participants an assignment that will require them to perform some action that applies these principles.

➕ **Life and Dignity of the Human Person**—Because all human life is sacred, we are called to treat all people with dignity. This principle is the foundation of the Catholic moral vision. We are called to respect and value people over material goods and to ask whether our actions respect or threaten the life and dignity of the human person.

➕ **Call to Family, Community, and Participation**—Our faith and our society rely upon healthy families and healthy communities. Because the family is the central social institution of our society, it must be supported and strengthened. When people have healthy families, they are better able to participate in society and to foster a community spirit that promotes the well being of all.

➕ **Rights and Responsibilities**—Not only does every person have a right to life, but also a right to those things needed for human decency. We are called to protect these basic human rights in order to build a healthy society. Each of us has a responsibility to protect those rights in our own everyday experiences.

➕ **Option for the Poor and Vulnerable**—It is a simple fact that, in our world, many people are very rich while, at the same time, many are extremely poor. We are called to pay special attention to the needs of the poor by following Jesus' example. We can do this by making a specific effort to ensure that those who are poor and vulnerable are able to meet their immediate material needs.

➕ **The Dignity of Work and the Rights of Workers**—Workers have basic rights that must be respected. These include: the right to productive work, to fair wages, to private property, to organize and join unions, and to pursue economic opportunity. Our Catholic faith teaches us that people do not serve the economy, but rather the economy is meant to serve people. More than being just a way to make a living, work is an important way in which we participate in God's creation.

➕ **Solidarity**—Because God is our Father, we are all brothers and sisters with the responsibility to care for one another. Solidarity is the attitude that leads Christians to share spiritual and material goods. Solidarity unites those who are rich with those who are poor and helps us to recognize our interdependence.

➕ **Care for God's Creation**—God is the creator of all people and all things and he wants us to enjoy his creation. Caring for all God has made is an important responsibility for all Catholics. We are called to make good choices—moral and ethical—that protect the ecological balance of all of God's creation.

One of my mentors, Fr. Jack Daley, taught me that every lesson in religious education must have a "so-what?" step. In other words, unless our learners can articulate concrete ways to live the lesson in their daily lives, the lesson is incomplete.

Glossary

Mentor—The word *mentor* is the name of a mythical character in *The Odyssey* who is a very wise guardian. We, too, are called to be wise guardians or guides to those we teach. The more trust we place in our participants, the more trust they develop in us. The mentor/apprentice relationship is based on and thrives upon this mutual trust.

Apprentice—The dictionary tells us that an apprentice is any beginner or learner who is bound to another for a fixed period of time in order to learn a trade, skill, or business. While this may sound formal, it really does apply. Our participants are bound to us for a fixed period of time, during which we hand on the knowledge and skills of discipleship that were handed on to us.

Troubleshooting

Teaching apprentices requires great patience. Sometimes apprentices can really "screw up." A good mentor knows how to offer correction without tearing someone down. If you place responsibility in the hands of one of your participants and are let down, take a deep breath, and handle the situation calmly but not sarcastically. Never criticize publicly. Rather, take your apprentice aside and offer correction and advice privately, all the while encouraging him or her to begin asking, "How will I do this differently next time?" because there will be a next time.

> "In the fulfillment of your duties, let your intentions be so pure that you reject from your actions any other motive than the glory of God and the salvation of souls."
>
> —ANGELA MERICI

"There—now I've taught you everything I know about splitting rocks."

Scripture

"For I received from the Lord what I also handed on to you, that the Lord Jesus, on the night he was handed over, took bread, and, after he had given thanks, broke it and said, 'This is my body that is for you. Do this in remembrance of me.'"

(1 CORINTHIANS 11:23–24)

Prayer

St. Paul was apprenticed ("I received . . .") and was now apprenticing ("what I also handed on to you . . ."). Thank you, Lord, for those mentors who apprenticed and continue to apprentice me as I struggle to acquire the knowledge and skills needed to live the gospel. Help me in turn, Lord, to apprentice my participants, to hand unto them that which I have received so that they may also become your disciples and live out the Good News of the kingdom of God.

For an opportunity to companion with other catechists and to nourish our vocation, visit www.catechistsjourney.com.

Conclusion: Looking for Results

Throughout this book, I have been making comparisons between tools used in home repair and the tools needed for effective catechesis. Many similarities exist. However, there is one major difference. Typically, when one completes some home repair, he or she can stand back and look at the final outcome, and take satisfaction in the tangible results. As a catechist, your results will be much less tangible. How does one know when a life has been touched, a soul has been stirred, or a spirit has been ignited? Most often you will not know the extent to which your lesson and your presence have been effective. In my own experience as a high school teacher, I recall a former participant coming back to see me many years after his graduation. He thanked me for a particular class session that I taught when he was a student. He said that it really came in handy now that he was in the workplace. I went home knowing that I had a good day some five or six years previous!

> "If God can work through me, he can work through anyone."
> —St. Francis of Assisi

Many of us will never know what effect we have had on our participants. For this reason, it is all the more crucial to focus on acquiring the tools needed to be an effective catechist. The more refined our skills are, the more keenly aware we will be to the effects of our lessons. The more specific we are about our own expectations of our participants, the more specific the results will be. We may never know just how much we have touched the lives of our participants. But, with the proper catechist's toolbox, we will leave our lessons knowing that—in some way—the Word of God *has* touched their lives. In the end, we must realize that we are simply a tool in the hands of the carpenter from Nazareth.

Appendix 1:
A Guided Reflection

The following example of a Guided Reflection (meditation) is from *Finding God: Our Response to God's Gifts*, Grade 5 (Loyola Press, 2005).

Called to Holiness

Time: approximately 10 minutes

We all have imagination. Imagination allows us to go places and to do things that might otherwise be impossible. Today we are going to use imagination to help us pray. *(Pause.)*

Now before we begin, find a position that feels most comfortable to you. *(Pause.)* If you like, close your eyes. *(Pause.)* Now relax your entire body—your neck . . . your shoulders . . . your arms . . . your legs. *(Pause.)* Feel all the tension flowing out of your body, into the air and away.

(Pause.) Now be very still and listen to the rhythm of your breathing. Listen. *(Pause.)* Feel your breath go in and out, in and out, in and out. *(Pause.)* Now let's begin. *(Pause.)*

In your imagination see yourself in a place where you'd like to be. Maybe it's a place where you've met Jesus before, maybe it's a different one. You choose, because anything is possible in imagination. Why not make it your favorite time of year? *(Pause.)* Make the weather suit you today. *(Pause.)* Be there in your imagination. Wait for Jesus to join you. *(Pause.)*

He does almost right away. As he comes in sight, you go to meet him. He's obviously glad to see you. Hear him tell you how glad he is to be with you again. *(Pause.)* As usual, he asks you what you were just doing. Sometimes your answer to that question would be, "Not much." But today it's different. He asks if you've been thinking about a verse from the Bible: "For I, the LORD, am your God; and you shall make and keep yourselves holy because I am holy."*

Now that's not your usual line of thought. But there's something in this verse that puzzles you. You don't have trouble with the idea of *God* being holy. But the idea of *you* being holy, of making and keeping yourself holy, well that needs a little more explanation.

Perhaps Jesus asks you to think of qualities that you would use to describe God—maybe qualities such as loving, forgiving, patient, understanding, generous, and so on. Let's call these "God qualities." Then he asks you to think of someone you know who has some God qualities. Who is it? Tell Jesus about this person. *(Pause.)*

Jesus, a great storyteller himself, might ask you to share a story about this person. It may take some time to choose just one story, but that's OK. Take the time to remember and then share your story with Jesus. *(Pause.)*

Jesus explains that God is all-holy. He tells you that you are holy when you act in a God-like manner. When you live your life with generosity, understanding, patience, then you are holy. Yes, *you! You* are *holy.*

What an awesome statement. Now think about that. *(Pause.)* Do you tell Jesus that being holy is what you want, but you're a little bit worried about being able to live up to that calling? *(Pause.)*

As usual, Jesus is reassuring. He wants you to know that you don't become holy all at once. You grow in holiness. You'll make mistakes but that's OK. You can always learn from them and try again. He reminds you that the Holy Spirit is always with you to guide you. Jesus says that he himself will help you anytime you need him. *(Pause.)*

Does that make you feel better? *(Pause.)* Go with Jesus now deep down into your heart. You've discussed a lot with him already, so now just rest in his love. Words are no longer needed. Be still together. Know how much he cares for you. *(Pause.)*

You recognize that it's time to go now. If you want a special blessing from Jesus, just ask for it. Remember to thank him, and then say good-bye. *(Pause.)*

Gradually bring yourself back to the room. *(Pause.)* Straighten up. *(Pause.)* Stretch. *(Pause.)* Plant your feet firmly on the floor. *(Pause.)* Look all around you. *(Pause.)* Everyone's here. We're all back.

* *Scripture citation in this reflection is Leviticus 11:44.*

Appendix 2:
Reliable Catholic Web Sites

There are many other reliable Catholic Web sites available on the Internet besides those on this list. Here are some helpful navigational hints.

◆ Start with official Web sites sponsored by your parish or diocese, other dioceses or religious communities, the US Catholic bishops, and the Vatican.

◆ Check out the suggested links on those Web sites to see what they recommend.

◆ When exploring a Web site, read the "about us" page to see who sponsors it and what they stand for.

◆ Cross-check your sources to ensure that the information is accurate or to explore a variety of interpretations.

◆ Avoid any Web site that contains offensive material.

The following list was compiled by Sr. Julie Vieira, IHM, and Joe Paprocki.

4 Catholic Educators—A portal to information on the Catholic faith and to resources for teachers, catechists, directors of religious education, and pastors. http://4catholiceducators.com/

Archdiocese of St. Paul and Minneapolis—Catholic social teaching documents and related information can be found on this site. www.osjspm.org/cst

Bible Gateway—This is a service for reading and researching Scripture online. www.biblegateway.com

Bible Search: Revised Standard Version—This Scripture search engine helps locate words and phrases in the Bible. www.hti.umich.edu/r/rsv

Catechism of the Catholic Church—The entire text of the Catechism, including a search engine, concordance, and glossary appear here. www.vatican.va/archive/ccc/index.htm

Catechist's Journey—Joe Paprocki, author of *The Catechist's Toolbox*, shares reflections on the experience of serving as a catechist for eighth graders. www.catechistsjourney.com

Catholic Book Publishers Association—Contact information for Catholic book publishers in the United States and abroad is readily available.
www.cbpa.org

Catholic Campaign for Human Development—The CCHD helps people to rise out of poverty through empowerment programs that foster self-sufficiency.
www.povertyusa.org and www.usccb.org/cchd/

Catholic Catechist—A source for comprehensive teaching resources for catechists and teachers.
www.catholiccatechist.org

Catholic Charities—Their agencies help families and individuals overcome tragedy, poverty, and other life challenges.
http://www.catholiccharitiesinfo.org/

Catholic Church Extension Society—This society works to sustain and extend the Catholic faith in poor and remote mission areas of the United States.
www.catholic-extension.org

Catholic Music Network—This is an extensive source for Catholic music on the Internet.
www.CatholicMusicNetwork.com

Catholic News Service—The CNS reports the news that affects Catholics in their everyday lives.
www.catholicnews.com

Catholic Online—Information about Catholicism can be found on this site, along with an online historical and biblical database.
www.catholic.org

Catholic Relief Services—The CRS is the official international relief and development agency of the US Catholic community.
www.crs.org

Creighton University Online Ministries—Creighton University offers resources in the Catholic prayer tradition and in Ignatian spirituality.
http://www.creighton.edu/CollaborativeMinistry/online

Daily Word of Life—This site provides daily meditations based on the Mass readings of the Catholic Church as well as memorials of the saints, prayer, news, events, home Bible study, and more.
www.daily-word-of-life.com

FindingGod.org—Loyola Press offers a wealth of information and resources for Catholic catechists.
www.FindingGod.org

New American Bible—This is the official online version of the New American Bible.
www.usccb.org/nab/bible

Patron Saints Index—An alphabetical index (including profiles) of patron saints can be found here.
www.catholic-forum.com/saints/indexsnt.htm

Religious Ministries Online Guide—This site offers a guide to discerning vocations as well as a database of Catholic ministries and religious and lay communities.
www.religiousministries.com

Resources for Catholic Educators—Resources for Catholic catechists and teachers.
www.silk.net/RelEd

Second Vatican Council Documents—The full text of the sixteen major documents of the Second Vatican Council can be found here.
www.vatican.va/archive/hist_councils/ii_vatican_council/index.htm

Theology Library at Spring Hill College (The Jesuit College of the South)—This site contains links to numerous Church documents and periodicals on a variety of theological topics.
www.shc.edu/theolibrary/index

United States Conference of Catholic Bishops—This is the official Web site of the US Catholic bishops.
www.usccb.org

The Vatican—This official Web site of the Vatican includes the Catechism and other church documents.
www.vatican.va

Vision Vocation Network for Catholic Vocation—This guide includes links to religious communities as well as listings of discernment, service, and educational opportunities.
www.visionguide.org

God's Library
A Catholic Introduction to the
World's Greatest Book
ISBN-13: 978-0-8294-2069-2
ISBN-10: 0-8294-2069-X
5 1/4 x 8 Paperback
160 Pages
$13.95

In *God's Library,* Joe Paprocki, a veteran catechist and Bible authority, guides readers into a basic understanding of "God's Library"—the collection of seventy-three books that Catholics regard as the definitive written revelation of God.

In easy-to-understand language, he explains the organization of the Bible, the different genres of biblical writing, key figures in biblical history, and the methods Catholics have developed to interpret the Bible properly. He shows beginning readers how to use commentaries, concordances, footnotes and cross-references, and other valuable tools of Bible study.

God's Library will delight all Catholics who are beginning their journey to read God's Word.

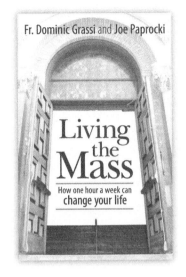

Living the Mass
How One Hour a Week
Can Change Your Life
ISBN-13: 978-0-8294-2076-0
ISBN-10: 0-8294-2076-2
5 x 7 Paperback
208 Pages
13.95

"We are meant to live the Mass, not merely attend it," write Fr. Dominic Grassi and Joe Paprocki, a priest and a layman who fervently believe that the central worship event of the Catholic faith is meant to transform our world. They begin their book by quoting the words that the priest says at the end of every Mass "Go in peace to love and serve the Lord." This outward-looking, service-oriented focus is the purpose of the Mass. It is intended to equip Catholics with the grace, knowledge, and energy to heal a broken world.

In their lively, readable explanation of the Mass, the authors are particularly alert to the way the Mass strengthens and renews the baptismal commitment of those who attend. Catholics are not strangers to each other but are a body of brothers and sisters, redeemed by Christ, and charged with carrying out his continuing work in the world. The Eucharist is food for a journey of service to family, community, and the world.